# YANKEE DOODLES

# YANKEE DOODLES

## INSIDE THE LOCKER ROOM WITH MICKEY, YOGI, REGGIE, AND DEREK

## PHIL PEPE

Sports Publishing books may be purchased in bulk at special discounts for sales promotion, corporate gifts, fund-raising, or educational purposes. Special editions can also be created to specifications. For details, contact the Special Sales Department, Sports Publishing, 307 West 36th Street, 11th Floor, New York, NY 10018 or sportspubbooks@skyhorsepublishing.com.

Sports Publishing® is a registered trademark of Skyhorse Publishing, Inc.®, a Delaware corporation.

Visit our website at www.sportspubbooks.com.

10 9 8 7 6 5 4 3 2 1

Library of Congress Cataloging-in-Publication Data is available on file.

Cover design by Eric Kang
Front cover photo: AP Images
Back cover images by Ed Murawinski

ISBN: 978-1-61321-762-7
Ebook ISBN: 978-1-61321-785-6
Printed in the United States of America

# CONTENTS

# Prologue

*WHEN I WAS A BOY MY GREATEST JOY*
*WAS GOING TO A BALLGAME.*
*I COULD HARDLY WAIT FOR THE APPOINTED DATE*
*COUNTING HOURS 'TIL THAT DAY CAME.*
*AT NIGHT I'D DREAM OF MY FAVORITE TEAM*
*THEY WERE THE BROOKLYN DODGERS.*
*JACKIE AND DUKE, PEE WEE AND NEWK*
*AND A BIG GUY NAMED GIL HODGES*
*MY MOM WOULD PACK A TASTY SNACK*
*BUT I HARDLY HAD TIME TO EAT IT.*
*THE GAME FLEW BY WITH THE BLINK OF AN EYE*
*AND SOON IT WAS TIME TO BEAT IT.*
*I'D SCREAM AND SHOUT 'TIL THE FINAL OUT*
*AND USE UP ALL MY HANKIES*
*WE CRUSHED THE CUBS, ALL NL CLUBS*
*WHY COULDN'T WE BEAT THE YANKEES*
*NOW I'M A MAN AND STILL A FAN*
*BUT THE GAME I FEAR IS CHANGING*
*PLAYERS WAIT, THEY PROCRASTINATE*
*WHAT ARE THEY REARRANGING?*
*THEY SCRATCH AND PAW, THEY SPIT AND CLAW*

*NO WONDER THEY NEED A SHOWER.*
*IT'S HARD TO BEAR AND NOW I SWEAR,*
*THEY MUST BE PAID BY THE HOUR.*

My love affair with this game called baseball began when I was six. I started following my Brooklyn Dodgers through the warm, soft, syrupy, southern tones of Red Barber, "the Old Redhead," pouring like molasses through my radio, and by checking the box scores in my morning newspaper. I saw my first game at Ebbets Field on May 8, 1942 (my Dodgers of Dolph Camilli, Pete Reiser, PeeWee Reese, Joe "Ducky" Medwick, Arky Vaughn, and Billy Herman beat the New York Giants of Mel Ott, Johnny Mize, Billy Jurges, and Dick Bartell 7–6; I was hooked), and my first no-hitter on April 23, 1946, pitched against the Boston Braves by a Dodgers pitcher with the unlikely name of Ed Head, who won only two other games that season and had a career record of 27–23 for five major league seasons, all with the Dodgers; and I cajoled my aunt to teach me long division before it was taught in school so that I could figure out batting averages.

This love affair continues to this day, some seven decades later, and remains ongoing, for better and for worse.

The "worse" is interleague play, the designated hitter, the wild card, five-man pitching rotations, managing by computer, umpiring by television replay, free agency, pitch counts, "quality starts" defined as going six innings and surrendering three earned runs, pitchers who rarely finish what they start, three-and-a-half-hour games, Velcro (why must *every* batter after *every* pitch step out of the batter's box, unfasten the Velcro on his gloves, and then refasten it before getting back in the box, thereby adding countless minutes to the length of the game?), and relief pitchers, or "closers," who don't report for work until the ninth inning.

The "better" is that the game itself has changed little over the past almost two centuries. It's still basically the same game that was invented by Abner Doubleday—or Alexander Cartwright, or Bobby Valentine, or Tony LaRussa, or Billy Beane.

Imagine the foresight and genius of the framers of this great game who placed the bases ninety feet apart, the pitching rubber sixty feet, six inches from home plate, deployed nine men on a side, established the length of a game at nine innings and decreed that each half-inning shall consist of three outs.

The game of baseball must be great to have survived the fools that have run it. It is great because it is particularly unique, made so by nine (notice the symmetry here!) reasons baseball stands apart from the three other major team sports.

- Dress Code: Baseball is the only sport in which the manager (or coach) wears the same uniform as the players (thank heaven we have been spared the sight of Red Auerbach, Rick Majerus, and Lou Carnesecca in short pants).

  The reason baseball insists on managers dressing like the players is that a manager is not allowed on the field in street clothes—but unlike in the other major sports, managers often spend time on the field talking to pitchers during the games. Since all participants must be dressed uniformly (hence the term "uniforms"), the managers must be dressed like the players.

  In baseball there have been two notable exceptions. Connie Mack, who managed the Philadelphia Athletics for fifty-three years (he won a record 3,778 games and lost a record 4,025) and was a part owner of the team, sat in the dugout wearing a suit, a high starched collar and tie, and a hat. He was not permitted on the field.

He sent a coach dressed in a uniform to the mound to make pitching changes, which produced one of my favorite stories, courtesy of Bob Lemon.

Mack had a pitcher named Louis Norman (Bobo) Newsom, who toiled for twenty years in the major leagues with nine different teams (including two hitches with the Athletics, 1944–46 and 1952–53) in the days when there were only sixteen major league teams. Bobo was one of baseball's most endearing characters, an angry, ornery right-hander who won 211 games and lost 222 and left his mark as a character. Four times in his career he started both games of a doubleheader.

On the mound, Newsom fought with everybody, including his own teammates. He hated being taken out of a game, a chore that Connie Mack avoided by being dressed in street clothes. So to deliver the bad news to Bobo, Connie Mack sent a coach to the mound, usually Mack's righthand man, his son, Earle.

One day Bobo was getting hammered all around the lot, and the more he was hammered, the more ornery he became. When Connie Mack could no longer witness the carnage, he sent his son Earle out to remove Bobo from the mound, a message that Earle Mack knew would be taken less than kindly by Newsom.

Fully expecting Newsom to explode and bite his head off, Earle approached the mound cautiously. He confronted the pitcher, shuffling his feet as he contemplated the proper way to break the bad news.

"Bobo," the sixty-something coach said finally, "*Daddy* wants you to come out of the ballgame."

The only other manager to work without a uniform was Burt Shotton, who was chosen by Branch Rickey in 1947, Jackie Robinson's rookie season, to lead the Brooklyn Dodgers after Leo Durocher was suspended for consorting with known gamblers. Shotton dressed in street clothes except for a Dodgers warm-up jacket and won pennants in 1947 and 1949.

- No Return Policy: Unlike football, basketball, and hockey, a baseball player may not reenter a game once he is replaced by a substitute.

- Time Stands Still: Baseball is the only major team sport that does not employ a clock. Consequently, in theory, unlike other team sports, no lead is insurmountable in baseball. A 4-touchdown lead in football with 2:00 to play, or a 20-point lead in basketball with :24 remaining, or a 5-goal lead in hockey with a minute left leaves the trailing team helpless and hopeless. In baseball, a team behind in the score can overcome any deficit; it can keep scoring indefinitely, and the game isn't over until the trailing team overcomes the lead or the last man is out.

- Different Strokes for Different Folks: Football fields, basketball courts, and hockey rinks are pretty much standard in size and shape. Not so with baseball, where the playing surface can vary from Fenway Park's Green Monster in left field to McCovey Cove in AT&T Park, to Yankee Stadium's short right field porch and cavernous expanse in center field. It's a different game, for instance, when the Yankees and Red Sox play in Fenway Park than when they play in Yankee Stadium. As a result, teams will tailor the makeup of their roster to the contours of their home ballpark (i.e., right-handed sluggers and right-handed pitchers for the Red Sox, left-handed sluggers and left-handed pitchers for the Yankees).

- No Place Like Home: There is no coin flip in baseball, no jump ball, no face-off. The home team gets to bat last in each inning and, most important, in the final inning.

- All Teams Are Created Equal: In football, one team can conceivably maintain possession of the ball for forty minutes and the other team for twenty minutes. In basketball, one team can take 50 foul shots and the other team can take 15. In hockey, one team can fire 40 shots on goal and the other team can have 6 shots on goal. Not so in baseball. Each team gets the same number of innings in which to score, nine, and the same number of outs, three per inning, or twenty-seven for the game.

- Defense Rests: Baseball is the only major team sport in which a team cannot score when the opposition is in possession of the ball (or bat).

- Pitch and Woo: The most important player on the team (the pitcher) does not play in every game. Imagine the Chicago Bulls without Michael Jordan, the Denver Broncos without Peyton Manning, or the Boston Bruins without Bobby Orr. The Yankees were a better team, had a better chance to win when Mariano Rivera was on the mound than when Hideki Irabu was on the mound.

- Star Search: Is there another team sport in which the star player and leading box office attraction cannot control a game or influence its outcome? Can you imagine a football game in which Joe Montana didn't throw a pass or Jim Brown never carried the ball; a basketball game in which Lebron James didn't take a shot or Bill Russell never grabbed a rebound; a hockey game in which Wayne Gretzky didn't touch the puck? In baseball, it's conceivable that Miguel Cabrera can be walked four times and never get to swing the bat and Derek Jeter can play the entire nine innings at shortstop and never have a ball hit to him.

Those are just nine, of many, reasons that baseball is unique among major team sports—nine reasons I love it and wouldn't have it any other way.

On the pages that follow I will endeavor to pour out all the passion for the game I have loved all of my life and to recount many of the stories I have accumulated in the more than twenty years of covering the New York Yankees.

# ONE

# MR. YOGI

"Hey, kid, whaddya doin'?"

The voice—coarse, familiar, and gravelly—was unmistakable.

The year was 1959. It was late in July, and I was about to fulfill a long-held ambition to travel with and cover a major league baseball team for a New York newspaper, the late and lamented (unfortunately by too few of us) *World-Telegram & Sun*.

Only one thing was missing. The team I was about to cover was not the one I had fantasized about covering when I was a child. My beloved Brooklyn Dodgers were no longer. They existed only in my heart and mind and in my dreams, having slipped through my fingers and transplanted across the country. Although I did manage to cover one game in fabled Ebbets Field, I had missed by a mere two years my goal of traveling with "Dem Bums." Instead, the baseball gods had perpetrated a cruel joke on me. My fantasy would have to be fulfilled by covering the hated Damn Yankees.

It was past the midpoint in the season when I got my big break and the Yankees were struggling to stay above the .500

level, a circumstance I would have relished in my Dodgers-loving, Yankees-hating younger days.

This was to be a trip for what was known in baseball as "scrubeenies" (i.e., backup players who rarely had the opportunity to shine). The other writers representing New York's eight daily newspapers on this trip were not the regular Yankees beat writers but rather disenfranchised baseball writers (they had regularly covered the Dodgers and Giants) or young upstarts like me. Furthermore, the Yankees would be traveling without their fabled and legendary manager, Casey Stengel, who was ill, depriving me of the joy of getting to know the inimitable Casey and listening to him weave his storehouse of fascinating tales told in his peculiar and unique form of fractured English. Managing the Yankees on this trip would be "the Major," Coach Ralph Houk.

Alas, I rationalized my sad fate with the knowledge that the Yankees were the only team in town and that at least it was baseball.

My dad (a New York Giants fan and, like me, suffering baseball withdrawal) drove me to Grand Central Station, where I would board the team sleeper train to Cleveland (the Yankees' traveling secretary at the time was Bill McCorry, an old spitball pitcher who appeared in two games with the 1909 St. Louis Browns and who apparently had a fear of flying). I had never been on a sleeper before, but I managed to make myself comfortable and prepare for sleep. I dutifully followed instructions and placed my shoes in a designated compartment. I was dumbfounded when I awoke the next morning to discover my shoes had been shined. How did that happen? Where did the railroad find someone small enough to fit into that compartment?

Another eye-opener for this rookie traveler was arriving in Cleveland early in the morning, boarding the team bus that took us to the team's hotel, and having my luggage delivered directly to my room without ever having to touch it.

Once I had settled in—what, you mean I have to unpack my own bag?—I ventured down to the hotel lobby to pass the time until the bus was scheduled to leave for Municipal Stadium for that night's game.

So there I was wandering aimlessly around the lobby of the aptly if unimaginatively named Cleveland Hotel when I heard the familiar voice—"Hey, kid, whaddya doin'?"—and I turned around and looked into the beautifully homely face of one Mr. Berra, of all people—the Number One name on my all-time hate list.

For years I found it difficult to forgive him for continually breaking my teenaged Brooklyn Dodgers–loving heart in the World Series (a .429 batting average in the 1953 World Series for example; 3 home runs, 10 runs batted in, and a .360 batting average in the 1956 World Series). I was guilty of blasphemy. I despised the man.

*"Bless me Father, for I have sinned. It has been two New York Yankees world championships since my last confession.*

*"I ate meat on Friday.*

*"I disobeyed my parents.*

*"I fought with my brothers.*

*"I hate Yogi Berra."*

My earliest encounters with His Yoginess were cursory ones back when I was an unbelievably young, unbelievably naïve reporter. Many people called me by my last name. They had since I was a kid. It was short, catchy, and easy to remember. I would occasionally be assigned to Yankees games in search of a feature story to augment my newspaper's game coverage. After a few visits to Yankee Stadium I suppose Berra came to recognize my face and, I assumed, knew my name, so I was somewhat more comfortable when my sports editor sent me to Macy's Department Store to do a story about Berra signing copies of his newly published autobiography.

I welcomed the assignment and also the gift from the publisher, a copy of the book, which I asked Yogi to sign. He graciously agreed to do so, and with pen in hand he scribbled on an inside page "To Pepe." Suddenly he stopped writing, looked up at me, and asked, "Hey, what's your last name?"

It was an epiphany. I didn't realize it at the time, but I had personally experienced my first Berraism. I also didn't realize there would be more, a whole lot more through the years.

But that day in Cleveland, there was only "Hey, kid, whaddya doin'?"

I gulped hard and managed to blurt out something inane like: "NOTHINGJUSTKILLINGTIMEUNTILIHAVETOLEAVE-FORTHEBALLPARK."

"Take a walk," he said (commanded?) "I gotta buy a birthday present for Carm."

I assumed, and eventually learned, that "Carm" was Carmen, the lovely Mrs. Berra.

So there I was with Yogi Berra, the guy I hated, the guy who broke my teenage heart again and again, walking across the street to Higbee's Department Store and to the elevator, which we took to the lingerie department. I could hardly wait to get back to my hotel room, call home, and tell my folks, "Guess who I just went shopping with."

It was, you might say, the start of a more than half-century acquaintance with the lovable, inimitable Mr. Yogi (since we didn't socialize or hang out and our interaction was primarily that of reporter to player/coach/manager, I don't dare be so presumptuous as to call it a "friendship," but I like to think that would be how he would describe it).

It wasn't long before I realized I had done the man a disservice. Despise Yogi Berra? It's not possible to dislike this humble, self-effacing, down-to-earth teddy bear of a man.

My more than a half-century relationship with Yogi is ongoing and in that time I must have written at least a half million words about him and repeated several hundred stories and Yogisms. I have taken the equivalent of an advanced course at Berlitz, passed with flying colors, and become proficient in YogiSpeak. I have learned to cut through the malapropos and mispronunciations to get at the root of his words in order to understand exactly what he meant to say. Once one has mastered that technique, making sense of Yogiese is simple.

For example, when he famously said of a Minneapolis restaurant, "Nobody goes there anymore, it's too crowded," what he meant was that the "nobody" he referred to was his crowd of Yankees teammates.

Consider his logic when one spring he wore a different color sweater every night and boasted that in his closet he possessed every color sweater except "navy brown." (If dark blue is navy blue, then dark brown must be navy brown. Makes sense to me.)

Yogi was managing the Mets when he came up with the often-quoted, "It ain't over 'til it's over," his simplistic way of saying you can't fold your tent and quit on a game or a season until you are mathematically eliminated.

It was while managing the Mets that Yogi was approached by the veteran Hall of Fame longtime St. Louis Cardinals broadcaster Jack Buck, who in addition to his play-by-play work was committed to do a pregame show during which he interviewed players, coaches, managers, and other baseball dignitaries. As compensation for giving their time, Buck's guests would receive a check for $25 (this was in the early 1970s when $25 was worth something). Because Buck was constantly traveling with the team and couldn't get to his office, he carried a handful of checks with him each made out "Payable To Bearer."

Buck asked the irrepressible Yogi to be his pregame guest and the always gracious Yogi agreed. Buck conducted his interview, thanked his guest, handed him a check, and began to walk away.

Yogi looked at his check and shouted to Buck to come back.

"Hey," Yogi said, "how long do you know me?"

"I don't know," Buck replied. "Maybe twenty or twenty-five years."

"You know me twenty-five years," Yogi said, "and you still don't know how to spell my name."

After he had been fired by the Yankees in 1985, Berra was invited by his New Jersey neighbor and good friend Dr. John McMullen, owner of the Houston Astros, to join the team as a bench coach. He settled into his new team, new league, and new life, and one day I called to check on how he was adapting to life in Texas. In the course of a long and rambling interview when I mentioned his unique use of the language, he commented, "I didn't say all the things I said."

In fact, he *didn't* say all the things he said.

Many wild and wacky quotes attributed to him were concocted by Jackie Farrell, a tiny man with a quick wit who had been a boxing writer for a New Jersey newspaper before serving for many years as director of the Yankees Speakers Bureau. Other contributions to YogiSpeak were made by Joe Garagiola (Berra's childhood pal and neighbor and a Hall of Fame broadcaster and humorist) and an army of advertising copywriters.

In the interest of total disclosure I freely admit to being guilty of perpetuating the Berra myth by repeating many of these stories over the years and passing them off as authentic. However, on these pages I vow to repeat only those comments I have heard with my own two pair of eyes, as you-know-who might say.

**BILLY MARTIN'S DILEMMA:** The Yankees manager was in a quandary. He was frustrated. He was angry. He was helpless. He had arrived at Fort Lauderdale Stadium one morning during spring training, parked his Lincoln Mark V in the lot adjacent to the stadium, and headed for the manager's office. It wasn't until sometime later that Martin realized he had locked his keys in the car.

As a product of the streets—he grew up in Berkeley, California—Martin would have had a simple solution to the problem: find a wire coat hanger (readily available in any closet), straighten the hanger leaving a loop at the bottom, and stick the hanger into the car through the window on the driver's side. Hook the loop onto the button that unlocks the door and pull.

But there was a problem. Martin's new luxury automobile was theft-proof. It was impossible to get a wire hanger into the car through a window. Consequently, when coach Yogi Berra arrived and entered the manager's office he found Martin in distress.

"Whatsa matter Billy?" Berra asked.

"Awww, I locked my keys in my car and I can't get a wire hanger down the window. I don't know what to do."

"That's easy," Berra proclaimed. "You gotta call a blacksmith."

**HAPPY BIRTHDAY:** Yankees coach Joe Altobelli was celebrating a birthday.

"How old are you?" asked his pal, Yogi Berra.

"Fifty," Altobelli said.

"Oh, you're an old Italian scallion."

**BARBECUED RIBS:** In perusing Yogi Berra's background one day, I came across the amazing fact that in his first professional season with the Norfolk Tars of the Class B Piedmont League he had driven in 23 runs in a doubleheader. I was aghast. I thought it might make an interesting story if I asked Yogi what he remembered about the day, whether he could explain how he was able to accomplish such a remarkable feat.

Of course he could. One doesn't forget driving in 23 runs in two games. His recollection was vivid.

"Every time I came up," he revealed, "there were men on base."

**KEEPING TABS:** Yankees manager Yogi Berra was parched. After a lengthy session during spring training on a humid Florida afternoon he came off the field huffing and puffing as he slumped down on the sofa in his office.

"Hey, Nick," he called to clubhouse attendant Nick Priore, "bring me a diet Tab."

**DAGGONE IT:** Before Jay Leno there was Johnny Carson. Before Johnny Carson there was Jack Paar. Before Jack Paar there was Steve Allen. And before Steve Allen there was Jerry Lester, a vaudeville comedian who served in the 1950s as host of the first late-night variety television show, *Broadway Open House*, the forerunner of *The Tonight Show*.

A regular on *Broadway Open House* was a statuesque, five feet, eight inches tall, amply endowed blonde from West Virginia who went by the stage name "Dagmar." With her eye-popping statistics of 42-23-39, Dagmar was the show's most alluring personality and television's first major female star.

Coincidentally, the Yankees in 1960 had instituted a policy in which a disabled youngster was invited to a game as a guest of the management and was escorted before the game to position himself outside the Yankees' clubhouse where players might stop and sign an autograph or chat briefly with the child.

One Sunday afternoon the youngster was a boy in his early teens who was confined to a wheelchair. He was accompanied by his twenty-something amply endowed blond sister, which conjured up for Yogi Berra remembrances of a similarly constructed female.

As he left the clubhouse Berra caught a glimpse of the young woman, did a double take, turned to look at a reporter, and exclaimed, "Who's that DAGWOOD?"

**GONE FISHING:** On a recent visit to the Yogi Berra Museum and Learning Center on the campus of Montclair State University in Little Ferry, New Jersey, I engaged the individual for whom the center is named in a rather lengthy, far-reaching, and nostalgic discussion on all things baseball. I mentioned to Mr. Berra that I had been watching a game on television involving the Texas Rangers and I had seen Rangers manager Ron Washington sneak off to take a quick drag on a cigarette.

That led to a discussion about managers smoking in the dugout. Berra had been a smoker in his managing days, and he confessed to sneaking off during a particularly stressful situation to grab an occasional butt. He had long since quit the habit, but he recalled that Earl Weaver, manager of the Baltimore Orioles, secreted a package of cigarettes in his uniform shirt and would frequently sneak down the runway to light up.

The practice of smoking in the dugout has diminished considerably in recent years, but there still had been some who were unable to kick the habit, like Ron Washington and Jim Leyland, the veteran manager of the Detroit Tigers.

"Oh, Leyland," Mr. Yogi agreed. "He smokes like a fish."

# TWO

# PROFESSOR

The baseball-writing press that had been summoned to New York's elegant "21" Club on October 12, 1948, was stunned—most of them, anyway—when the Yankees revealed the identity of the man they had chosen to replace the popular Bucky Harris as their manager. He was Charles Dillon Stengel, better known as "Casey," in recognition of his birthplace, Kansas City, Missouri. The consensus of the writers was that the Yankees had made a terrible mistake.

The new man was too old—he would turn fifty-nine during the 1949 season.

The new man had no previous connection to the Yankees—he managed nine years in the National League and played his entire fourteen-year career in the National League with the Dodgers, Pirates, Phillies, Giants, and Braves. He did, however, oppose the Yankees as a member of the Giants in the 1922 and '23 World Series, batting .417 and .400, respectively. In the '23 Series Stengel hit a ninth-inning game-winning home run off Sad Sam Jones in

Game 1 and a seventh-inning game-winning home run off Bullet Joe Bush in Game 3.

The new man had no previous success as a major league manager—in fact he was an utter failure as a manager with both the Brooklyn Dodgers and the Boston Braves/Bees, posting one winning record in nine seasons, finishing no higher than fifth place, and logging a combined winning percentage of .439. In Boston, he was so despised that he was under the constant and merciless attack of the sports columnist of the *Boston Record,* the acerbic Dave Egan, known as "the Colonel." In 1943, Stengel had been struck by a car prior to opening day, causing him to miss the first two months of the season with a broken leg. Summing up the '43 season, Egan wrote: "The man who did most for baseball in Boston in 1943 is the motorist who ran Stengel down two days before the opening game and kept him away from the Braves for two months."

Despite a respectable lifetime batting average of .284 as a player for his 14 major league seasons to go along with 60 home runs and 535 runs batted in, the new man was looked upon as a clown by the baseball establishment, Yankees co-owners Dan Topping and Del Webb included. What seemed to define Stengel was a series of antics such as strolling into the batter's box one day, doffing his cap, and setting a sparrow free.

It was Yankees general manager George Weiss who, over the objections of Topping and Webb, championed the selection of Stengel to succeed Harris. Weiss had known Stengel for some forty years and regarded him as a knowledgeable baseball man, one who ate, slept, and breathed the game and would talk about it for endless hours. Weiss maintained that in Boston and Brooklyn, Stengel was hamstrung by inferior talent. Weiss pointed to the fact that Stengel had done a remarkable job the previous season in winning the Pacific Coast League championship with the Oakland ballclub.

At a time when owners put up their money and then stepped aside and let their baseball people make the baseball decisions, Topping and Webb acquiesced to Weiss, clearing the way for Stengel to come aboard as the sixteenth manager of the New York Yankees.

If the selection of Stengel was met with skepticism among the fans, the writers had another opinion. The writers who had known Stengel as a player and as a rival manager were fond of the former aspiring left-handed dentist. "If you didn't like Casey Stengel you didn't like anybody," said John Drebinger, the long-time and well-respected Yankees beat writer for the *New York Times.*

The writers were pleased to have a personality like Stengel to provide them with stories. They enjoyed his unique, colorful, and archaic manner of speech, which soon would become known as Stengelese. In Stengelese nothing ever started or began—it "commenced"; nobody was fired or let go—he was "discharged"; everyone who came in contact with him, close friends, former teammates, and members of the media, was called "Doctor," a remedy to avoid insulting people because Stengel rarely remembered names and those he did remember he frequently misspelled or mispronounced.

What the writers traveling with the Yankees knew, the general public would find out on the afternoon of July 8, 1958. In nearby Baltimore for the annual baseball All-Star game the day before, Stengel was summoned to Washington, DC, to testify as an expert witness at the Senate Anti-Trust and Monopoly Subcommittee hearings chaired by Senator Estes Kefauver. What resulted was pure, unadulterated Stengelese.

Senator Kefauver (Democrat, Tennessee): "Mr. Stengel, you are the manager of the New York Yankees. Will you give us very briefly your background and views about this legislation?"

Stengel: "Well, I started in professional baseball in 1910. I have been in professional ball, I would say, for forty-eight years. I have been employed by numerous ball clubs in the majors and in the minor leagues. I started in the minor leagues with Kansas City. I played as low as Class D ball, which was at Shelbyville, Kentucky, and also Class C ball and Class A ball, and I have also advanced in baseball as a ballplayer. I had many years that I was not so successful as a ballplayer, as it is a game of skill. And then I was no doubt discharged by baseball, in which I had to go back to the minor leagues as a manager. I became a major league manager in several cities and was discharged. We call it discharged because there is no question that I had to leave."

Senator Kefauver: "Mr. Stengel, are you prepared to answer particularly why baseball wants this bill passed?"

Stengel: "Well, I would have to say at the present time I think that baseball has advanced in this respect for the player help. That is an amazing statement for me to make because you can retire with an annuity at fifty and receive money. I want to further state that I am not a ballplayer that is put into the pension fund committee. At my age, and I have been in baseball well, I would say I am possibly the oldest man who is working in baseball. I would say that when they start an annuity for the ballplayers to better their conditions it should have been done and I think it has been done. I think it should be the way they have done it, which is a very good thing. The reason why they possibly did not take the managers at that time was because radio and television or the income to ball clubs was not large enough that you could have put in a pension plan. Now I am not a member of the pension plan. You have young men here who are, who represent the ball clubs, they represent the players. And since I am not a member and don't receive pension from a fund which you think my goodness he ought to be declared in that too, but I would say that is a great thing for the ballplayers. That is one thing I will say for the ballplayers, they have an advanced pension fund. I should think it was gained by radio and television or you could not have enough money to pay anything of that type.

"I have been up and down the ladder. I know there are some things in baseball thirty-five to fifty years ago that are better now than they were in those days. In those days, my goodness, you could not transfer a ball club in the minor leagues, Class D, Class C ball, Class A ball. How could you transfer a ball club when you did not have a highway? How could you transfer a ball club when the railroad then would take you to a town you got off and then you had to wait and sit up five hours to go to another ball club?"

Senator Kefauver: "Mr. Stengel, I am not sure that I made my question clear."

Stengel: "Yes, sir. Well that's all right. I'm not sure I'm going to answer yours perfectly either."

Senator Kefauver: "I am asking you, sir, why is it that baseball wants this bill passed?"

Stengel: "I would say I wouldn't know, but I would say the reason why they'd want it passed is to keep baseball going as the highest-paid baseball sport that has gone into baseball and from the baseball angle. I am not going to speak of any other sport. I am not here to argue about other sports. I'm in the baseball business. It has been run cleaner than any baseball business that was ever put out in the hundred years at the present time."

Senator William Langer (Republican, North Dakota): "I want to know whether you intend to keep monopolizing the world's championship in New York City."

Stengel: "Well, I will tell you. I got a little concerned yesterday [in the All-Star game, won by Stengel's American Leaguers, 4–3] in the first three innings when I saw the three players I had gotten rid of [former Yankees Jackie Jensen, Bob Cerv, and Gus Traindos batted third, fourth, and seventh in the AL lineup] and I said when I lost nine what am I going to do? And when I had a couple of my players I thought so great of that did not do so good up to the sixth inning [three Yankees—Mickey Mantle, Bill Skowron, and Yogi Berra—were a combined 1 for 9 until Gil McDougald singled home what proved to be the winning run in the bottom of the sixth] I was more confused but I finally had to go and call on a young man in Baltimore [left-hander Billy O'Dell, who retired the National League in order in the last three innings] that we don't own and the Yankees don't own him and he is doing pretty good and I would actually have to tell you that we are more the Greta Garbo–type now from success. We are being hated. I mean from the ownership and all we are being hated. Every sport that gets too great or one individual—but if we made twenty-seven cents and it pays to have a winner at home why would you have a good winner in your park if you were an owner? That is the result of baseball. An owner gets most of the money at home, and it is up to him and his staff to do better or they ought to be discharged."

Many years later, I was working on a book about Yogi Berra and I telephoned Stengel to ask him about the man he once described as "my assistant manager." I asked one question and received a nonstop reply. Here is part of his response:

"Yogi Berra worked for me a long time, and when he started he had a wonderful career because he lived in St. Louis, which I was familiar with because I lived in Kansas City when I went to dental college, and he was living in Kerry Patch[1] because all the Irish was there; then in come the 'Eyetalians' like Graziola[2] and Berra and they commenced makin' more money because they worked in the factory and if it wasn't a factory they kept busy and everybody worked and they brought the beer in a bucket or whatcha call a pitcher that they filled because it was very hot in St. Louis like you wouldn't believe next to hell and the fellows was very tired in the factory and finally they got started with the ball club and most of the players like Howard[3] lived there and for thirty to forty years they played ball in three or four parks[4] when the National League had it.

"Now Berra became very well known when the war commenced because Phil Rizzuto was in the navy in Portsmouth and immediately Berra went and joined and this is when I wasn't there he wanted to sign up with the Yankees and he came to see the business manager and if you went there you had to go through two or four secretaries, but he had four or five things that he could do which wasn't funny to me in my life with his antics. He was very nervous when he was there and young and now he has raised three kids that are taller than he is, every one of them . . . he had a way of walking around you know like a bear and they forgot that he could bat like Graziola did and you could

---

[1] The section in St. Louis where Berra grew up, now called the Hill, was known as Kerry Patch in earlier days when it was inhabited by Irish immigrants.

[2] Joe Garagiola.

[3] Former Yankees catcher Elston Howard also was a native of St. Louis.

[4] The St. Louis Browns joined the American League in 1902 and left in 1954. The St. Louis Cardinals have been in the National League since its inception, playing home games in several ballparks, including Sportsman's Park and Busch Stadium.

look it up that he went up there and he didn't care about signs if you tell him to bunt and he swung and hit some of them for home runs and you can't catch home runs . . ."

And that was just the beginning. A few minutes and several hundred words later, he was still talking about Berra . . . I think. "One year he [Berra?] had stopped hitting, not stopped but he had bad luck and he coulda led the league in home runs except he pulled the ball too much.[5] They slowed up on him and I'd jump out and I'd say 'Oooohhh, it's foul but it will be a home run' and he had beautiful brilliance with writers about why he hit bad balls for home runs you better not throw the ball over the plate to him. 'Yeah,' I said. 'I'd like to see 'em throw the ball over the plate too he'd do pretty good.'

"I always thought he worked good with young pitchers. That's why he could beat that Cleveland club eighteen times without ever losing a game if you look it up. Now when you talk about [Whitey] Ford he was the best pitcher we ever had for a left-hander and they used to say he [Berra again?] didn't think good and I said 'Huh, huh,' but he hits good and he rearranged the Dodgers and they were scared to death that he would hit to left field and they made a great catch and there went Mr. Stengel[6] . . .

---

[5] A reference to Berra's habit of repeatedly pulling balls four into the right field seats in Yankee Stadium.

[6] A sensational one-handed catch by Brooklyn Dodgers left fielder Sandy Amoros on a ball hit by Yogi Berra with two on and nobody out in the bottom of the sixth inning of Game 7 of the 1955 World Series prevented the Yankees from tying the score. After a long run, Amoros turned what looked like a certain game-tying double into a double play. The Dodgers went on to win the game, 2–0, and their only World Series in Brooklyn. It also was the Brooklyn Dodgers' only World Series victory over the New York Yankees in seven tries.

"He had good instruction from Dickey and he got better. He's an awkward man but he's fast. When we beat them in Brooklyn and they had all those good managers like Durocher and Dressen he's the one [who] went out and got the ball and they called him out but he could go out and get the bunt. Another thing he did when he was playing he never showed he was going crazy on the field you never saw him tearin' up a uniform did you? But I don't want to tell you too much about him because then you'll have five thousand pages."[7]

---

[7] You'd better believe he would.

# THREE

# THE YANKEE CLIPPER

He was the embodiment of Yankees grace, elegance, dignity, and class. He was the "perfect" ballplayer. When people talk about the Mount Rushmore of Yankees baseball, it is clear who the first three members are (though the fourth may be up for debate)—always it's Babe Ruth, Lou Gehrig, and "Joltin' Joe" DiMaggio, the "Yankee Clipper," who was immortalized in story—

*"'I would like to take the great DiMaggio fishing,' the old man said. 'They say his father was a fisherman. Maybe he was as poor as we are and would understand.'"*—Ernest Hemingway in *The Old Man and the Sea*.

He was also recognized in a song recorded in 1941 by Les Brown and his Band of Renown.

DiMaggio's signature accomplishment and defining moment was, of course, his 56-game hitting streak, a record that has endured more than seven decades and likely never will be broken, but there also are his .325 lifetime batting average, the three Most

Valuable Player awards, and the seven consecutive seasons with more than 100 runs batted in, a streak that was terminated by three years in military service in the midst of his halcyon days during World War II.

Yet the true measure of his greatness was this:

In 1941, he batted .357, hit 30 home runs, drove in 125 runs, walked 76 times, came to bat 622 times, and struck out just 13 times.

For his career, he played in 1,736 games, hit 361 home runs, and struck out 369 times.

His achievements were not lost on several other legendary ballplayers, either:

"Ted Williams was the greatest hitter I ever saw, but Joe DiMaggio was the greatest all-around player."—Bob Feller

"Joe DiMaggio was the greatest all-around player I ever saw."—Ted Williams

"As one of nine men, Joe DiMaggio is the best player that ever lived."—Connie Mack

"He's the most complete ballplayer I've ever seen."—Joe McCarthy

"There was never a day when I was as good as Joe DiMaggio at his best. Joe was the best, the very best I ever saw."—Stan Musial

Unlike some of these men, who witnessed this greatness firsthand, though, I didn't know DiMaggio when he was a player. I was a year old when he joined the Yankees, a high school senior when he played his last game. I saw him play several times, but I regret that when he was at his best I was too young to appreciate his grace and talent and when I was old enough to appreciate those things, he was no longer at his best.

I got to know him years after he retired when he returned as a legendary hero to Yankees events, for special occasions, to spring training, and Old Timers Days.

I learned early on to tread carefully in the presence of the great man. Any acknowledgment, question, or discussion of his marriage to the actress and sex goddess Marilyn Monroe, even the mere mention of her name, resulted in immediate and lifetime banishment from his circle, eternal inclusion in journalistic purgatory regarding all matters DiMaggio. A similar fate awaited any failure to worship at his pinstriped shrine or to acknowledge the magnitude of his playing career.

I understood too that he did not like to be asked for autographs, but he would occasionally sign them under certain conditions and if shown the proper respect. So I bowed and scraped and gauged his moods and made a point to learn when it would be acceptable to ask for an autograph. I relished and wore as a badge of honor that he addressed me by name and that I was among the relative few who had earned his trust enough to ask for an autograph, always taking precautions not to abuse the privilege.

One such occasion came during the 1978 season. A New York City art gallery had produced a series of lithographs of famous major league baseball stadiums. For publicity purposes, the gallery sent members of the media postcard-size replicas of the lithographs, and those postcards spurred an idea. My eldest son had started to collect baseball memorabilia. My plan was to mount two of the postcard replicas with different views of Yankee Stadium onto a blue background and then obtain a silver pen and get as many current and former Yankees to sign in silver on the blue background. When I had completed my mission, I would frame the piece and present it to my son as a Christmas present.

I was the Yankees beat writer for the *New York Daily News* at the time, and I dutifully carried that piece around the country for two seasons. When I came in contact with a former Yankee,

I would ask him to sign my cherished souvenir (eventually I obtained the signatures of more than forty Yankees, including more than a dozen Hall of Famers).

As the second season of my mission—and my self-imposed deadline—was coming to an end, I was aware that of all the autographs I had collected, one critical one was missing; Joe DiMaggio. I vowed that I would not end my pursuit until I had secured the signature of (at the time) the greatest living ex-Yankee. I knew I would inevitably run across him sometime, I just didn't know when. But I wanted to be prepared when I did.

Finally, on Old Timers Day 1978, with my pet project in my possession, I walked into the press dining room and saw the Great DiMaggio sitting alone at a table. Cautiously and somewhat sheepishly and with some trepidation, I approached the Great Man, greeted him warmly, and waited for the proper moment to make my request.

"I have this piece," I stammered, "and I'm planning to give it to my son for a Christmas present and I would be honored if you would sign it for me."

"All right," he said with a hint of annoyance, I thought. "Let me see it."

I produced the carefully rolled-up piece, unrolled it, and laid it on the table in front of DiMaggio.

"That's very nice," he said.

Buoyed by his reaction, I pressed my advantage and made certain to emphasize that my intention was to give the piece to my son as a Christmas gift, not to sell it (at the time former players were beginning to resent autographing items that would eventually be sold without them receiving so much as a fee for their time and effort).

"Yes," I said. "I think it will make a nice Christmas gift, and I want to assure you that I have no intention of making a profit by selling the piece to a collector.

"In fact," I continued, "I don't even know if the piece has any real value."

As I said the words "any real value," Joe was finishing writing the "O" on the name "DiMaggio." As he did, he looked up and said, "It does now!"

# FOUR

# NUMBER 61

I had covered only a handful of major league baseball games for the *New York World Telegram & Sun* when I was abruptly and surprisingly summoned to the sports editor's office one day and informed that I would be taking over coverage of the New York Yankees.

You might say it was the journalistic equivalent of Wally Pipp's headache that brought this remarkable circumstance about. I was the unwitting beneficiary of an illness to a member of our staff. Joe Williams, our legendary brilliant sports columnist, was ailing and was expected to be out of action for several months. To write the column in his place, the sports editor promoted the longtime Yankees beat writer and the dean of New York baseball writers, Dan Daniel. That left the Yankees' beat open, and I was selected to fill it.

It was a watershed moment in my career. I was getting my big chance, my dream assignment. It wasn't my beloved Dodgers (they had left Brooklyn a few years earlier), but it was Major League Baseball, and it was the Yankees—at the time the most important and the most prestigious assignment on any New York sports page.

I was excited by the opportunity, and I proudly boasted to my sports editor that I was ready for the challenge. But was I really?

I had just returned from Boston, where I was part of my newspaper's team coverage of Major League Baseball's annual All-Star Game when I was informed of my new responsibility. Perhaps I was too naïve to realize the enormity of my task. Veteran baseball savants will have no such problem understanding what was facing me when I explain that my new duties were to begin on August 2, 1961. The Yankees were to start a nine-day, ten-game homestand with a game and a half lead in the American League.

But that was only part of the story.

I was being tossed smack dab into one of the biggest sports stories ever, the chase by Mickey Mantle and Roger Maris, the "M&M Boys" to headline writers, of the most celebrated of all sports records—the single season home run mark of the legendary, mythical, larger-than-life Babe Ruth.

I joined the party in time to see Mantle hit his 40th home run of the season in the first inning of the second game of a doubleheader against the Kansas City Athletics. The home run would tie his teammate and friend, Maris, for the major league lead.

Two days later, Maris clouted No. 41 against Camilo Pascual of the Minnesota Twins, and two days after that Mantle put on one of his typical power displays in a doubleheader with the Twins. He blasted two home runs in the first game against his old patsy, Pedro Ramos, and another in the second game against a journeyman right-hander named Al Schroll, and the race was on in earnest.

After chasing Maris through the months of May, June, and July, Mantle had finally caught his teammate and passed him, most observers thought for good. But it was not only Maris who Mantle was chasing, it was also Ruth, and it was not only Mantle who was chasing the Babe, it was also Maris. At the completion of the day's play on August 6, 1961, Mantle had 43 home runs and was 19 games ahead of Ruth's 1927 record pace, and Maris had 41 home runs and was 16 games ahead of Ruth's pace.

I had been around the Yankees often enough over the past year and a half that I had a relationship of sorts with both Mantle and Maris, tenuous at best as it was. At least they knew my face and I knew a little about them. But this was going to be different. I would be around them constantly, home and away, and I was going to be in their face on a daily basis. My mandate from my sports editor was that in addition to covering the game, I was to write about the M&M Boys every day regardless of whether they hit three home runs or struck out four times.

As such, I got to see up front and personal the many moods of both men.

I found Mantle to be an enigma. He could be gracious, charming, affable, cooperative, and humorous one day, and rude, crude, lewd, standoffish, and irritable the next. I noticed that he seemed to respect the veteran writers covering the team and was more accessible to them. But I had not been around long enough to have earned such treatment.

Maris was different. In the beginning, I found him to be cordial, cooperative, approachable, and relatively at ease. At the same time he spoke in a dull monotone with platitudes and clichés. He had very little to offer, but rarely was there an edge in his voice. He didn't smile often, but when he did it was a warm, welcoming smile that brightened a pleasant, handsome face that was crowned by a blond crew cut.

Maris was a small-town country boy, his itinerary a Rand-McNally odyssey of Midwestern farming and mining towns, born in Hibbing, Minnesota, raised in Fargo, North Dakota, residing in Raytown, Missouri. He began his major league career in Cleveland and was traded to Kansas City, where he hit 35 home runs in 258 games over two seasons and caught the Yankees' eye with his left-handed swing that they deemed tailor-made to attack the cozy right field fence in Yankee Stadium.

On December 11, 1959, the Yankees made Maris the key man in another of the endless, usually one-sided trades with the Kansas City Athletics, a seven-player deal that sent Yankees heroes Hank Bauer and Don (Perfect Game) Larsen to the Athletics along with Norm Siebern and Mickey Mantle–wannabe Marvelous Marv Throneberry, in exchange for Maris, infielder Joe DeMaestri, and first baseman Kent Hadley. The Yankees were thrilled with the trade. Maris was less so.

Maris would have preferred to remain in Cleveland or Kansas City, where he was building a home in the suburb of Independence, Missouri, the home town of President Harry S. Truman. He was uncomfortable in the big city, but his first year with the Yankees was a rousing success. He led the American League in RBI with 112, finished second in home runs, one behind Mantle, his more popular and more celebrated teammate, and was voted the AL's Most Valuable Player.

Despite all that, Maris somehow managed to fly under the radar that first year in New York, but now he was in a fish bowl, unable to hide, as he was locked with Mantle in a race to unseat the mighty Ruth as the all-time single season home run king.

Dealing with Mantle and Maris obviously was going to be a necessary evil for anyone covering the 1961 Yankees, but Mantle's hot-one-day-and-cold-the-next volatility and Maris's innate reticence coupled with my inexperience and lack of any lengthy relationship with either player indicated that this chore I had been handed was not going to be an easy one.

Fortunately, I had formed an easy friendship with Jim Ogle of the *Newark Star-Ledger*, the senior member of the cadre of Yankees beat writers and a man who would become not only a friend, but also a mentor. Ogle had formed a close bond with Maris, and that, inadvertently, eased my access to one of the two men of the hour. The more I was seen in Ogle's company, the more Maris became available to me. I also quickly discovered that the best way to engage Maris in pleasant conversation was to ask about his family. A few weeks after I joined the Yankees, on August 21, Maris's wife Pat gave birth to the couple's fourth child. When I asked Maris about the new addition, or about any of his three older offspring, he would soften perceptively and drop his protective, deadpan demeanor.

As time went on during the 1961 season and the controversy of his pursuit of Ruth escalated, several old-time players, led prominently by Rogers Hornsby, were outspoken in their belief that they deemed a .257 hitter like Maris (his lifetime average before the '61 season) unworthy to replace the great Babe Ruth as baseball's all-time single season home run king. Commissioner Ford Frick, a former sportswriter who had served as a ghostwriter for Ruth, succumbed to overwhelming pressure and decreed that because the major league schedule had increased that season from 154 games to 162, any player surpassing Ruth's record after the 154-game deadline would go into the books with an "asterisk" attached to make note of the fact that the deed was accomplished with the aid of an additional eight games. In turn, Maris became less approachable, more difficult to interview, and less quotable.

At the same time, as he got closer to Ruth's record, Maris would have to deal with writers from other cities who would arrive at Yankee Stadium. The crowd around Maris's locker would swell, leaving Roger even more irritable. Had this even come only a few years later, the Yankees would have reserved a private room in their clubhouse to be used for mass interviews, which is a custom practiced today on a daily basis. Instead, Maris had to face the media in front of his locker, which only added to his discomfort and to an infringement on his privacy.

Maris was continually besieged for interviews—everybody wanted a piece of him, and some even insisted on private, one-on-one interviews. He was constantly bombarded with questions about Ruth's record. He abhorred most of the questions. Consequently, he would answer them in his dull monotone, often curtly, sometimes grudgingly voice, and occasionally he would not answer them at all. One question even brought a rare display of levity to the situation.

A group of writers had gathered around Maris's locker on this particular occasion, among them a young man unknown by the regulars who covered the team. He would later identify himself as a college student from Texas who was there as a representative of his school newspaper. (How he was given credentials and by whom was never explained. Suffice to say it couldn't happen today.) The young interloper was not shy. During a lull in the interview session the young man from Texas asked Maris, "Would you rather hit sixty-one home runs or bat three hundred?"

The question stopped Maris in his tracks. It seemed rhetorical, unworthy of a reply, perhaps even a joke. But the young man persisted.

Maris decided the proper response was to turn the tables on the questioner.

"What would you rather do?" he asked.

"I'd rather hit three hundred," said the young man from Texas.

To which Maris smiled incredulously and said, "To each his own."

As time went on and the heat from the home run chase intensified, I noticed how the stress affected Maris. In Detroit, he had one hit, a single, in nine trips to the plate in a double-header against the Tigers and took refuge in the trainers' room, off limits to the media, where he spent forty minutes visiting with his brother Rudy, who had driven in from North Dakota.

In Baltimore, teammates and writers traveling with the team noticed that patches of Maris's hair had fallen out. He visited a local doctor, who ruled out anything physical. Stress was the diagnosis.

More and more, Maris appeared tormented by the chase and uncomfortable with the unwanted attention it brought him. In Yankee Stadium he would sit in front of his locker or at the large old oak table in the middle of the clubhouse drinking coffee from a paper cup, chain-smoking unfiltered Camel cigarettes, and jiggling his legs nervously.

It was clear Maris was ill at ease with the attention he was receiving. He appeared to get no enjoyment out of being the center of attention. He would have preferred to be left alone to go about his business quietly and without fanfare. He didn't play for records or personal glory. His priorities were family, country, and team. He was among the most humble of stars. When he hit a home run there were no high fives, low fives, fist bumps, or chest thumps, no standing at home plate to watch the flight of the ball, no curtain calls, no displays of bravado of any kind—when he hit home run No. 61, he had to be pushed out of the dugout by his teammates for a curtain call by the 23,154 fans. To do any of those things would be disrespectful to the opposition and to the game; it would be demeaning to the pitcher—such was a sign of the times that players did not pose, prance, preen, or strut upon rounding the bases after hitting a home run. When he hit a home run Maris simply dropped his bat, bowed his head, and trotted, not too fast, not too slow, around the bases, and when he reached home plate he surreptitiously, almost embarrassingly, accepted the congratulatory hand of a teammate.

More than a half century has passed since the great home run race, and there still is misinformation and misconceptions about events that occurred during that remarkable season, much of it transmitted in the written word and in Hollywood celluloid. This misinformation has centered around the relationship between Maris and Mantle and the role of the media in the piece. Perhaps you had to be there for the daily excursion to understand the truth.

Rumors surfaced during the season that there was a discord between Maris and Mantle, or a sense of envy of one for the other brought on by the overwhelming desire to be the one to break Ruth's record. Such stories flew in the face of the fact that Maris and Mantle became close friends as well as teammates that season; that Mantle and Bob Cerv invited Maris to share their apartment in the borough of Queens, the three usually driving together to and from their apartment and Yankee Stadium, just a hop, skip, and a jump from the Bronx over the Triboro Bridge; that Maris often played the role of cook, preparing meals for the three in the apartment, or that they often ate out together at home and on the road.

Were they rivals? Certainly! But no more and no less rivals than any two friends competing for the same prize.

However, when Mantle came down with a virus and missed four games in late September (later he would be hospitalized with a hip infection—the result, we were told, of being punctured with a contaminated hypodermic needle), returned on September 23 to hit his 54th home run, but went hitless in three trips the following day and removed himself from the lineup because of his illness, he told Maris, "That's it, Rog. I'm through. It's all up to you now."

It was not just lip service. Mantle landed in the hospital, and he watched from his hospital bed when Maris hit his 61st home run, rooting as hard as anyone for his friend and teammate to break the record.

After they retired as players, Maris and Mantle drifted apart. Maris moved to Florida and began a new career as the owner of a Budweiser distributorship. Mantle took up the career of being Mickey Mantle, signing autographs at shows, serving as a goodwill ambassador for the New York restaurant in his name, etc. When he learned that his old teammate came down with cancer, Mantle reached out to Maris and stayed in constant touch with his old home run partner. And when Maris succumbed to his illness, Mantle was devastated. He flew to the funeral in Fargo to serve as a pall bearer and was visibly distraught over the loss of a friend.

"I always liked Roger and respected him as an all-around ballplayer, not just a home run hitter," Mantle once said. "He could hit, he could run, he could field, and he could throw. He was one of the smartest players I've ever seen. He had great instincts for the game. I never saw him throw to the wrong base or miss the cutoff man. And I never saw him thrown out taking an extra base."

High praise from Mount Olympus!

Because Hollywood needs a villain, Billy Crystal's otherwise excellent made-for-television film *61*\* about the Mantle-Maris home run chase, decided it should be the writers covering the team, depicted as rooting against Maris in the race, wanting him to fail.

I was there. It was not true.

What was true is that Maris could be difficult and exasperating. He was bland and uninteresting and not, in the vernacular of the business, "a good quote."

But he was rarely uncooperative, and he was never hostile.

There no doubt were writers who considered Mantle more worthy to break the record because of his years of service with the Yankees and his glowing résumé, and who would have preferred that he be the one to break the record. But those preferences were never aired publicly. I never witnessed any overt rooting for Mantle (or against Maris) either in the press box or in private conversations with my colleagues.

I also believed it would be appropriate that Mantle break the record, but I tried not to hold that against Maris, and when Mantle appeared to run out of time, I hoped Maris would break the record. Why wouldn't I? It was good for business. It would sell newspapers.

Logic suggests that any writer covering the Yankees in the 1961 season, especially a young writer, would want to see someone, anyone, break Ruth's record, would want to be a chronicler of baseball history. It was one of the great accomplishments the game has known, and I feel privileged to have been witness to it.

# FIVE

# BUS STOP

There was a time, not very long ago, when baseball writers were accepted as part of a team's traveling party. They were welcomed—in fact, encouraged—to fly on the team's charter airplane, were included on the team's hotel rooming list, and shared bus rides with the players to and from airports and hotels and between hotels and ballparks. This occasionally resulted in an embarrassment for the team as writers on the bus were privy to, and freely reported, controversies, feuds, and even altercations between teammates they witnessed on the bus. (One notable exception was the tabloid beat writer who purposely failed to report a fight between teammates on the bus not out of a sense of loyalty or respect for the players' privacy but because "If I wrote about the fight my paper would know I rode the bus and wouldn't approve my use of a taxi on my expense account.")

The teams were happy to provide the service for the explicit purpose that it enabled them to bill the various newspapers for the writers' expenses as a means of helping the teams defray travel costs. That is no longer the case.

Baseball teams today generate so much income that they no longer need the newspapers' nickels and dimes to help make ends meet, and the players don't want the writers around any longer than is necessary. So the writers are not welcome on the team's charter airplanes or on the team bus. They are forced to make their own travel arrangements and their own hotel reservations usually in a hotel other than the one that houses the team. And they must walk, run, or taxi between hotels and ballparks on the road, thereby eradicating what once was for writers a fertile source of pertinent inside information, controversy, and humor.

How sad to contemplate that had this current practice been in effect years earlier, some of the game's most enduring and entertaining stories may never have come to light.

## NO HARM(ONICA) DONE

The Yankees had just been swept in a four-game series against the White Sox in Chicago, a potentially fatal blow that dropped them 4½ games out of first place with 43 games to play. It also left their rookie manager, the normally easy-going Yogi Berra, in a foul mood as he entered the team bus waiting to take the Yankees to Chicago's O'Hare Airport, where they would board a charter for their trip to Boston to meet the Red Sox in what was now a crucial four-game series.

Enter one Phil Linz, a backup shortstop and a blithe spirit, the sort who regaled the media one spring training with a story of how he was stopped for speeding by a member of the Fort Lauderdale police department. The officer proceeded to ask the motorist for his license and registration, which Linz produced as requested.

While perusing the documents, according to Linz, the officer noticed something.

"This says you need glasses," said the officer. "You're not wearing glasses."

"Oh," Linz explained, "I have contacts."

To which, according to Linz, the officer replied, "I don't care who you know. You're still getting a ticket."

Now, in Chicago, Linz was about to find himself embroiled in a major crisis. A few days earlier he had purchased a harmonica for the purpose of fulfilling a long-held ambition to master the instrument. He climbed onto the bus, took a seat in the rear, and dug out his new toy and the rudimentary instructions designed for the beginner. The song he chose to begin his career as a musical virtuoso was "Mary Had a Little Lamb," and he somehow thought that waiting on the bus after his team had lost four consecutive games was the proper time to further his musical studies.

Linz tootled and Berra bristled.

"Hey, Linz," Berra shouted. "Take that harmonica and stuff it."

Absorbed in his various clefs and rests, Linz didn't hear what Berra said, so he addressed others on the bus.

"What did he say?"

"He said play louder," offered Mickey Mantle.

Linz obliged. And Berra exploded.

"He started toward me," Linz later explained.

"Hey, Linz," said Berra. "I told you to take that harmonica and stuff it."

With that Linz flipped the harmonica to Berra and said, "Do it yourself."

According to Linz, "Yogi caught the harmonica and threw it back at me, but it hit Joe Pepitone on the leg. First there was silence and then all hell broke loose. Pepi is limping around and yelling that he's injured, and I jumped on the back of the seat and began shouting.

"Why are you yelling at me? I give you one hundred percent all the time. Why pick on me? Why not pick on some of these other guys who aren't hustling?'

"I don't know why I did it. I was uptight. I had been benched after I had a ten-game hitting streak, and I broke my neck for him whenever I played. I don't know. The harmonica was there and I just did it. It was an hour after the game. I didn't think it was so terrible."

It took a superstar like Mickey Mantle to make light of the incident and ease the tension. Seeing the harmonica laying on the floor, Mantle picked it up and announced, "Well, gang, that's it for our manager. From now on, I'm the manager. Here's the signal for a bunt . . . *toot!* Here's the signal for a steal . . . *toot, toot!*"

With that, everybody aboard the bus began to laugh, Berra included, and that was the end of the incident, until it hit the newspapers the following day.

In Boston's Fenway Park, Berra called a repentant Linz into his office.

"I'm sorry, Yog," Linz said. "I shouldn't have done it. I was wrong. You know I always give you one hundred percent."

"OK," Berra said. "But I gotta fine you."

"I know."

"It's gonna cost you two hundred fifty dollars."

"That's fair; sure," said Linz.

"And that's all there was to it. It was over, forgotten, just like two friends having an argument and putting it in their past. I never had any problems with Yogi before or after that incident. He was always very nice to me. When I was a rookie he used to take me out to dinner. He was a fantastic guy, but I guess he had his problems as a rookie manager and trying to manage the guys he played with and the club going bad. He was under a lot of pressure."

(P.S. After the four-game sweep by the White Sox in Chicago, the Yankees lost the first two games in Boston to run their losing streak to six. But they came back and Berra rallied the team to win 30 of their last 41 games and finish one game ahead of the White Sox to win the 1964 American League pennant. They lost the World Series to the St. Louis Cardinals in seven games, but after the Series, the Yankees fired Berra and replaced him with Cardinals manager Johnny Keane.)

"Later, when I joined the Mets and Yogi was a coach there we kidded about the harmonica thing and we even posed for pictures with me playing a harmonica. There never have been any hard feelings. That's the kind of guy Yogi is. He did what he had to do and it was forgotten."

After the 1964 season, Linz signed his Yankees contract for a healthy raise and a bonus of $200.

"For harmonica lessons," announced general manager Ralph Houk.

## STATIONARY STATIONERY

The bus was parked outside Yankee Stadium waiting to take the Yankees to the airport for the trip to St. Louis and the start of the 1964 World Series. Everything was ready, players and equipment and, yes, the writers, all on the bus. Only Bob Fishel, the team's able and affable Director of Public Relations, was missing.

Pitcher Jim Bouton had asked Fishel if there were any more World Series tickets available, and Fishel said he thought he might be able to dig one up and dashed into his office. A few minutes later, a breathless Fishel arrived and hopped aboard the bus. He was triumphantly brandishing a manila envelope, which he handed to Bouton.

"Boy, are you lucky," Fishel said. "This was the last one."

"What?" exclaimed manager Yogi Berra incredulously. "You mean they're outta them manila envelopes already?"

## ON THE DOTTED LINE

In almost twenty years of chronicling Yankees baseball, I found no player more of a joy to cover than Sparky Lyle, not only for his singular success as a relief pitcher but also for his pleasant nature, his affability and availability, and his weird and wacky sense of humor. He never saw a game, or a day, he didn't like.

From his penchant for sitting nude on birthday cakes to throwing his signature slider (he boasts that he pitched in 899 games in 16 seasons, won 99 and saved 238, and threw only one pitch; he could have gotten his signs from Captain Hook), nobody had more fun than Lyle, the guy with the Fu Manchu mustache.

What set Lyle apart was his demeanor. He was never too high or too low, always the same congenial, fun-loving loco lefty, win or lose. But don't think he was all fun and games when he took the mound.

He joined the Yankees in a trade from the Boston Red Sox in 1972 and left after the 1978 season when he was traded to the Texas Rangers. In between, he made his mark (on the field and in my notebook) in those seven years in pinstripes with 57 wins and 141 saves. He won the American League Cy Young award in 1977 and led the league in saves in 1972 with 35 and again in 1976 with 23 in an era when a "closer" was expected to pitch more than one inning and enter a game with runners on base and the game on the line.

A case in point was the 1977 American League Championship Series against the Kansas City Royals, his finest hour/hours as a Yankee. On October 5, he came in to record the final out in a 7–2 defeat. On October 7, during Game 3 in Kansas City, he pitched 2⅓ innings in a 6–2 loss that sent the Yankees one defeat from elimination.

On October 8 in Game 4, he allowed no runs and two hits in 5⅓ innings and was the winning pitcher as the Yankees squared the Series at two games each with a 6–4 victory.

Twenty-four hours later he was on the mound again, pitching 1⅓ innings and getting the win in a 5–3 victory that sent the Yankees to the World Series for the second straight year.

For me, however, Lyle's greatest Yankees moment came on the team bus parked outside the ballpark in Chicago waiting to head for O'Hare Airport. Suddenly the door opened and onto the bus popped an attractive twenty-something young woman, her blond hair flowing freely. She jiggled when she walked and seductively pleaded for autographs from the players, who were eager to comply.

The young woman produced a pen, but one player noticed she had no paper.

"Where are we going to sign?" he asked.

No problem, assured the woman as she turned her back to the crowd and deftly and quickly lowered her blue jeans to display an inviting target for their signatures. The rush to grant the wish of such a loyal fan was something akin to the bulls running at Pamplona. Consequently the woman's collection of signatures would make any autograph hound proud.

Later, I asked Lyle if he was among those that signed there.

"Of course," he eagerly replied. "I signed 'Albert Walter Sparky Lyle Junior.'"

# SIX

# SACRED BOVINE

It takes the mere mention of the name Phil Rizzuto to lighten my heart and bring a smile to my face. I hear it and I immediately think of cannoli, holy cows, huckleberries, on-the-air restaurant plugs, and birthday greetings to anyone he ever met or hoped to meet or who sent him a note—all of it at the expense of the action on the field, which he often neglected in order to make sure to mention the birthday greetings and plugs—and early exits from Yankee Stadium across the George Washington Bridge to beat the traffic and get home to his beloved Cora.

I think of hours he spent on the road watching movies on television (his favorite was Alfred Hitchcock's *North by Northwest*, which he claimed to have seen more than a dozen times) and of the morbid, irrational fear of flying, lightning, and things animate and inanimate that slime, creep, squiggle, and crawl. (I once mentioned to Bill "Killer" Kane, the droll traveling secretary of the Yankees, that Rizzuto had a fear of dying, to which Kane replied, "If you lived the life he's lived, you'd be afraid of dying too.")

I think of his naiveté, his ability to poke fun at himself and to admit to ignorance of some fact or some recently arrived player. I remember one airplane flight late in the 1976 season. I was sitting in the row behind Rizzuto talking with a Yankees pitcher. When the pitcher left his seat to go to the lavatory, Rizzuto turned to me and asked, "Who's that writer you were talking to?"

"That's no writer," I answered. "That's Larry Gura. He joined the team three months ago."

I think of his riotous, rollicking, hysterical, rambling, discombobulated 29 minute, 37 second Hall of Fame acceptance speech in which he grabbed the huge audience with his opening words: "Holy cow!"

He went on to say that the only reason he was there in Cooperstown for his induction to the Hall of Fame was "because of you fans, my family, my relatives, and all my friends. Wait a minute. No, really, I think you put so much pressure on them, kept sending in those petitions and saying, 'He should be in the Hall of Fame,' and actually my records paled with all these great Hall of Famers behind me, and that huckleberry Lou Brock—he keeps calling me a rookie. I'm the oldest living rookie in the Hall of Fame. I mean you talk about it taking a long time to get here."

Rizzuto went on to say he owed so much to his high school coach who "taught me how to bunt. Without knowing how to bunt I'd have never made it to the big leagues. Paul Krichell, a Yankee scout, signed me up to [Casey] Stengel, and Bill Terry told me I was too small to play baseball and that was a big break for me."

And he talked about his start in baseball when the Yankees "signed me to a contract and they sent me to Bassett, Virginia, in 1937. I'd never before been away from home. My father took a twenty-dollar bill and pinned it to my undershirt.

He said, 'You gotta watch out for those guys on the trains,' and the Yankees gave me a nice seat, no sleeper, sat all the way to Bassett, Virginia . . . Now Bassett was a town of sixteen hundred counting the cows. I got off the train, and there was no town there. I'm looking around at mountains just like the beautiful mountains, and then the train pulled away and there was the town. A little drug store, a theater that was only open two days a week, and a drug store, and that was the town of Bassett."

He reminisced about his time in the navy during World War II and how he would get seasick on the ferry.

From the podium he introduced his family, including "my pride and joy," the beauteous Cora, his wife, who talked him out of leaving the Yankees and signing with the Pascal Brothers from Mexico who in the 1940s raided the United States of major leaguers in an attempt to establish in their homeland a league to rival the major leagues. They offered untold riches, which tempted Rizzuto, but Cora, at personal sacrifice, convinced him not to be a traitor.

Unfortunately, many of us in the audience that steamy summer day in Cooperstown never saw him play—Rizzuto played his last game more than a half century ago—but we know about the 1950 American League Most Valuable Player award, and we know, from listening to our predecessors and to his peers—Joe DiMaggio, Tommy Henrich, Johnny Pesky, and Ted Williams, who often said the Red Sox, not the Yankees, would have won all those championships in the 1940s and '50s "if Rizzuto was our shortstop."

Most of us know him as a broadcaster—he spent more years (forty) announcing Yankees games than he did playing in them (thirteen, not including three years in the navy) as the brilliant, diminutive, high-energy, endearingly-named Scooter—but few of us had the pleasure and privilege of traveling with him, spending time with him, sharing experiences with him. I consider myself fortunate to have been one of those few.

He was the most self-effacing of men, a rarity among many of his contemporaries in what became his second career because he never took himself seriously. Rizzuto on the air was exactly what Rizzuto was off the air. Naïve! Childlike! Unpretentious! What you saw was what you got. As a traveling companion Scooter was a delight who made an often tedious and difficult job more tolerable.

When I think of Scooter Rizzuto I remember the on-air malapropos and observations that were so uniquely him. My all-time favorite is when he said: "There's [American League umpire] Larry Napp dusting off home plate from Staten Island."

I remember looking at Rizzuto's scorecard one day and noticing the letters "WW" spread all over it.

"What's WW?" I asked.

"Wasn't watching," Scooter replied.

I remember a game in Detroit, the Yankees against the Tigers on Sunday, June 24, 1962, a time when the Yankees traveled with only two announcers, Rizzuto and Mel Allen, who would switch between radio and television at the midpoint of the game.

On this day, the game would go twenty-two innings, and once the switch of announcers was made, each was trapped for the remainder of the game. And so it came to pass that Rizzuto, the Scooter, was on the radio and at about the 16th or 17th inning, as the Scooter was calling the action on the field, nature was calling him. Unable to leave the broadcast booth, Rizzuto had no choice but to find relief by putting an empty paper coffee cup to emergency use.

I repeat these stories not to embarrass him, but to emphasize what a genuine, unpretentious, humble person Phil Rizzuto was.

Traveling with him, knowing him, and spending time with him was one of the joys of more than twenty years of covering and traveling with the Yankees, and the thought that I will never hear him again, never spend time with him again, never poke fun at him again, never laugh at his idiosyncrasies again leaves a void than can never be filled.

I especially remember one particular rainy afternoon in Minnesota when several Yankees players and writers, looking to kill a few hours, decided to take in the popular X-rated movie *Deep Throat*. Rizzuto was invited to join the group, but he declined.

"Oh, no," he said. "I can't be seen at something like that."

Off we went to the theater, Scooterless. We were seated in the dark for about an hour when on the screen flashed a particularly erotic scene. Suddenly from the back of the silent theater, from a slightly built older man wearing sunglasses and with the collar of his raincoat turned up and the brim of his hat turned down came a familiar shriek.

"Holy cow!"

# SEVEN

# EXTRA! EXTRA!

It could not have been easy being Elston Howard, a Yankees rookie, in 1955. That year, Elston was the only African American on the Yankees roster.

Of course, this was eight years *after* Jackie Robinson had broken baseball's color line and was playing in Brooklyn, in the same city as the Yankees and only about 20 miles away from Yankee Stadium. Shamefully, baseball's most successful, most prestigious, most admired, and most watched team was the thirteenth major league franchise to integrate.

Yankees apologists pointed out that Branch Rickey had admitted he signed Jackie Robinson (and soon after Roy Campanella, Don Newcombe, and Junior Gilliam) because he believed they would help the Dodgers win pennants and boost attendance. But the Yankees needed no such stimulus. In the eight years prior to the arrival of Howard, they had won six World Series. In the five years before Howard, they had drawn 8,674,134 customers to Yankee Stadium. The Indians with Larry Doby drew 7,281,703, and the Dodgers with Jackie Robinson drew 5,741,178 and were already in talks to move out of Brooklyn and to Los Angeles.

Nevertheless the Yankees recognized the wave of the future and told their scouts to find players of color with the caveat that they be "the Yankee type," whatever that meant. It was never spelled out, but presumably it was "work hard, do your job, stay out of trouble, and keep your mouth shut."

In the early 1950s, the Yankees had two players of color moving rapidly up the ladder in their farm system. Howard was one. He had been a high school star in football, basketball, and track (his high school had no baseball team, but it formed one in Elston's senior year after watching him excel on the sandlots of St. Louis, his birthplace). Several colleges, including Illinois, Michigan, and Michigan State, wanted him for football, but Elston was seduced by an offer of $500 a month to play for the Kansas City Monarchs of the Negro American League, the team that launched Jackie Robinson's baseball career.

The Yankees purchased Howard's contract from the Monarchs on July 19, 1950, but first Howard had to fulfill another commitment. He spent the 1951 and 1952 seasons in the United States Army. When he was discharged, the Yankees sent him back to Kansas City, but this time it was for Elston to play for the Blues, the Yankees' top farm team in the Class AAA American Association.

Howard's manager with the Blues was Harry Craft, and his teammates consisted of 21 players who made it to the major leagues. In his first year of minor league ball, Elston batted a respectable .286 with 10 home runs and 70 runs batted in.

The following year, the Yankees sent Howard to the Toronto Maple Leafs, an independent team in the Class AAA International League with no affiliation to a major league team, their reasoning being they were shifting Howard to catcher on a somewhat permanent basis and they had an up-and-coming young catcher named Gus Triandos they wanted to play full time in Kansas City. In addition the Yankees believed Toronto to be more accepting of black players than Kansas City would be.

Skeptics and those who continued to accuse the Yankees of racial bias charged that the real reason they switched Howard to catcher was that there he would be blocked by the incumbent Yogi Berra. How could the bleeding hearts accuse the Yankees of prejudice when the man keeping Howard from being a starter with the Yankees was a two-time Most Valuable Player recipient (he would win his third MVP plaque in 1955)?

Still, Howard went to Toronto determined to make the Yankees take notice. He accomplished his mission by batting .333, hitting 22 home runs, driving in 109 runs, leading the league in triples, and being named Most Valuable Player of the International League. Now the Yankees had no choice but to promote him to the big team in 1955. And they had to find a position for him.

On the same trail up the Yankees minor league ladder as Elston Howard was another black man, Victor Pellot Power, a native of Arecibo, Puerto Rico, who seemed to be on the fast track to Yankee Stadium. The Yankees had purchased Power's contract in 1951 from the independent Drummondville team of the class C Provincial League and sent him to Syracuse of the International League, where he batted .294. The following year he went to Kansas City, hit a robust .331 with 16 home runs and 109 RBI and played a remarkable if flamboyant first base.

His numbers would appear to have earned Power a promotion to the Yankees, which would have made him the first black player in their history. After all, the first baseman in the Bronx was Joe Collins, a left-handed hitter who batted .269 with 17 home runs and 44 runs batted in. Power might easily have beaten out Collins. In the least, he could have been a right-handed platoon at first base with Collins (the Yankees had no right-handed hitting first basemen, and Bill "Moose" Skowron had not yet arrived). Instead, the Yankees sent Power back for another year in Kansas City. With nothing to prove and not much else to learn, Power produced another sensational year for his résumé, a .349 batting average, 16 home runs, and 93 runs batted in.

Now the Yankees could no longer ignore Power. But would two consecutive sensational years in triple A be enough to warrant a promotion to the major leagues? It would, and it did, but not to New York. On December 16, 1953, Power was part of an eleven-player trade between the Yankees and the Athletics, then playing in Philadelphia.

Their critics charged the Yankees with prejudice, and there was enough evidence to make the case. Even their supporters speculated that the Yankees dropped Power because he was not "the Yankee type." He was too flamboyant in the field, a showboat first baseman who seemed to perform with a "watch me" attitude to get the attention of the crowd. There also were rumors, never confirmed, that Power preferred white women and might even have been married to one and that the Yankees considered that intolerable.

Power would go on to a twelve-year career with five teams, post a .284 lifetime batting average, hit 126 home runs, drive in 658 runs, make the All-Star team four times and win six Gold Gloves. Had he stayed with the Yankees, he might have given them superior play at first base for a decade. However on the downside, had he stayed with the Yankees we might have been deprived of the outstanding play, the good fellowship, and the sunny disposition of Moose Skowron.

To this day I have not seen a first baseman as acrobatic, flashy, flamboyant, and as brilliant a showman as Vic Power. I got to know him later in his career, and I found him to be anything but ostentatious and egotistical. He was, in fact, quite humble. And apart from his problems with the English language, he was an engaging, cordial, and completely accommodating fellow.

Elston Howard, on the other hand, had all of those qualities and more. He was "the Yankee type," an army veteran, a family man, a solid citizen, and a damn good player who "worked hard, did his job, stayed out of trouble, and kept his mouth shut."

Howard was the ultimate team player, willingly moving all around the field while waiting for the catching job to open. When finally his time had come, he played fourteen seasons, was named to the All-Star team ten times, and was a member of ten pennant winners and four World Series champions. He demonstrated his versatility by appearing in 1,138 games at catcher, 227 in left field, 85 at first base, and 42 in right field.

But his true calling was as a catcher, where he displayed exceptional defense (he won two Gold Gloves and shot down a remarkable 44 percent of runners attempting to steal in his career, including a spectacular 55 percent in 1962). Despite suffering the usual aches and pains and gnarled fingers normally associated with a career as a catcher, Howard managed an impressive record as a hitter for average (he batted .348 in 1961) and power (he belted 70 home runs over a three-year span of 1961–63 and was American League Most Valuable Player in '63).

When Stengel left in 1961 and his successor Ralph Houk, a former catcher himself, arrived, Houk saw in Howard the ability to take his place behind Berra and Bill Dickey in a long line of outstanding Yankees catchers. Houk gave Howard the bulk of the catching (he made 106 starts to 42 for John Blanchard and 15 for Berra) and Ellie was also a potent offensive force on the famed M&M (Mantle and Maris) team. His .348 average was second in the league to Detroit's Norm Cash (Howard did not have enough at bats to qualify for the batting title), and he hit 22 home runs and combined with two other catchers, B&B, Berra (22) and Blanchard (21), to hit 64 home runs, three more than Maris.

Blanchard was an interesting case, someone who was ahead of his time. If ever there was a born designated hitter whose swing was tailor-made for Yankee Stadium, it was the left-handed, dead pull-hitting Blanchard, an outstanding clutch hitter who hit more home runs (two) in the 1961 World Series than Mantle, Maris, or Berra.

It was Blanchard's mediocre defense that prevented him from becoming a big-time star as a Yankee, and finally that weakness caught up with him. On Sunday, May 2, 1965, the Yankees were beaten by the Orioles. Blanchard, who was the starting catcher for the Yankees, was hitless in three at-bats that day. After the game he was informed that he had been traded to the Kansas City Athletics. I have never known any player who loved being a Yankee more than Blanchard. He was so crestfallen by the news that it left him in tears as he talked to the press.

Trying to console him, I said, "Think of it this way, John. You always said you wanted more playing time; now in Kansas City you'll get your chance to play more."

"You don't understand," he blubbered. "I can't play."

It turned out Blanchard was an even better prognosticator than he was a player. He appeared in 52 games with Kansas City and batted .200 with two home runs and 11 RBI in 120 at bats. The Athletics sold him to Milwaukee, where he got in 10 games, came to bat 10 times, and had one hit, a two-run home run, and was released, never to play again.

Meanwhile, Elston Howard continued his success as the Yankees catcher. He soon became one of the most beloved Yankees of his generation—beloved not only by the fans but by his teammates as well. Whitey Ford, Mickey Mantle, Phil Rizzuto, Hank Bauer, Billy Martin, and Yogi Berra all numbered him among their favorite teammates, and all spoke of him with great affection after Howard's untimely death in 1980 at age fifty-one. Especially Berra!

When his playing career was over, Howard became a coach for a string of Yankees managers. Berra also was a coach at the time, and the two men were practically inseparable on road trips. Their bond was strengthened by their similarities—both were from St. Louis, both were catchers, both lived in New Jersey, and both were early risers.

It was during this time while serving as Yankees beat writer for the *New York Daily News* that I came to know and appreciate Elston Howard as a man of unmatched character, good nature, and thoughtfulness. He will always be on my list of all-time favorite Yankees, regardless of how short that list is.

Many mornings on the road, in Boston, Cleveland, Chicago, Detroit, or wherever, I would awaken and notice that my phone was lighted, informing me that there was something in my mailbox at the front desk. I would check with the desk clerk, and he would present me with a copy of that day's *Daily News*.

I soon learned that Elston Howard would awaken early, hours before me, go to the newsstand, purchase the *Daily News*, which he read over breakfast, and when he was finished he would take the paper to the front desk and ask the desk clerk to put it in my mailbox.

A small thing? Not to me, it wasn't. To me it was a considerate gesture from a most considerate man.

# EIGHT

# THE NAME GAME

On January 8, 2007, the Yankees made undoubtedly the worst trade in their hundred-year history, worse than Jay Buhner for Ken Phelps, worse than Stan Bahnsen for Rich McKinney, even worse than Roger Maris for Charlie Smith.

It wasn't a straight-up, man-for-man deal, but rather merely a swap of roster spots. On that day, the Yankees traded the Big Unit, Randy Johnson, back to the Arizona Diamondbacks for four players. To fill Johnson's spot on the roster, they signed as a free agent Doug Man . . . er . . . Doug Ment . . . you know, that left-handed-hitting first baseman who used to play for the Minnesota Twins and later went to the Boston Red Sox and caught the ball for the final out of the 2004 World Series that ended the famed "Curse of the Bambino" and gave the Red Sox their first World Series championship in eighty-six years and who stuck the ball in his pocket for a souvenir and refused to give it back to the Red Sox. That guy!

The trade had nothing to do with swapping the 280 wins of a pitcher destined to be elected to the Hall of Fame as soon as he is eligible for whatshisname's 59 home runs and .271 lifetime batting average in nine big league seasons. Nonetheless the trade would live in infamy with those who write or talk about the game.

"What, you mean you traded a Johnson for a Man . . . a Ment . . . a Mient . . . for a guy whose name looks like twelve letters that seem to have been thrown together at random in no sensible order? You must be kidding!"

It probably took until June or July for writers and broadcasters to get the hang of it, to commit to memory that the guy's name was spelled M-I-E-N-T-K-I-E-W-I-C-Z . . . and that it was pronounced exactly as it's spelled. In other words, "MAN-CAVE-ITCH."

Up to that time, in their more than one hundred years, the Yankees had more than 1,400 players appear in at least one major league game, from **A** (Abbot, Jim) to **Z** (Zuvella, Paul), and there have been some wonderful names among those 1,400.

There have been three palindromes and one guy whose name you swore when you saw it was a misprint (Kevin Mmahat).

The Yankees have had a **Burns** (George) and **Allen** (Bernie), an **Abbott** (Jim) and **Costello** (Dan), a **Rogers** (Kenny), and **Hart** (Jim Ray), but no Hammerstein.

They have had a **Winfield** (Dave), a **Wakefield** (Dick) and a **Whitfield** (Terry), who played left field, center field, and right field, respectively.

They have had a **Kane** (Frank) and **Ables** (Harry), a **Hill** (Glenallen) and **Dale** (Berra), a **High** (Hugh) and **Lowell** (Mike), a **Long** (Dale) and **Short** (Bill).

The Yankees have had a **Cook** (Andy), a **Baker** (Frank), a **Brewer** (Billy) a **Weaver** (Jeff), and a **Taylor** (Wade).

**Nixon** (Otis) and **Kennedy** (John) wore Yankees uniforms. So did **Washington** (Claudell), **Adams** (Spencer), **Madison** (Dave), **Monroe** (Zack), **Jefferson** (Stanley), **Bush** (Homer), **Ford** (Whitey), **Clinton** (Lu), **Johnson** (Cliff), **Wilson** (Enrique), **Hayes** (Charlie), **Taylor** (Zack), **Jackson** (Reggie), and **Truman** (Clevenger).

The Yankees have had a **Duke** (Carmel) and an **Earle** (Combs), a **King**man (Dave) and a **Queen** (Mel), a **Hamilton** (Steve) and **Burr** (Alex), a **Glenn** (Joe) and **Armstrong** (Mike), **Spikes** (Charlie) and a **Clete** (Boyer). They have had **Bliss** (Elmer) and **Love** (Slim), **Knight** (Brandon) and (Brian) **Dayett**, **Moore** (Wilcy) and **Les** (Channell).

They have had **Gibsons** (Paul and Sam) and **Martinez's** (Tino and Tippy), **Buckles** (Jess) on **Coates** (Jim), a **Kitt** (Howie) and a **Katt** (Jim).

What the Yankees have rarely had are players with names longer than ten letters. Up to that time the Yankees had had ten players with eleven letters in their last name (Assenmacher, Kamienicki, Messersmith, Peckinpaugh, Porterfield, Scarborough, Stankiewicz, Stottlemyre, Throneberry, and Wehrmeister), but only two others (Christiansen and Monbouquette) with twelve letters and only one with more than twelve letters, a name easy to remember, easy to spell, and easy to pronounce because they named a basketball team after him—Billy Knickerbocker.

And then along came Mientkiewicz with his twelve letters that looked like they came right off a chart in an optometrist's office. There was just one problem. If the new guy was to be their regular first baseman, the Yankees were going to need a backup for him, and there was nobody on the roster who could spell Mientkiewicz.

## STRANGE BEDFELLOWS

It's a pity these Yankees never played together. If they had, you can imagine some road secretary with a sense of humor pairing them up as roommates:

BELL (John) and HOWELL (Jay)
LEWIS (Duffy) and CLARK (Allie)
FRENCH (Larry) FREY (Lonnie)
FRIEND (Bob) and BUDDIE (Mike)
HOLMES (Darren) and WATSON (Bob)
REED (Jack) and WRIGHT (Ken)
YOUNG (Curt) and OLDring (Rube)
LOCK (Don) and KEY (Jimmy)
MARTIN (Billy) and LEWIS (Jim)
MASON (Jim) and DIXON (Sonny)
MOORE (Archie) and MOORE (Wilcy)
HALL (Mel) and OATES (Johnny)
HUNT (Ken) and PECK (Steve)
PROCTOR (Scott) and GAMBLE (Oscar)
ELLIS (John) EILAND (Dave)
ASHFORD (Tucker) and SIMPSON (Harry)
RICE (Harry) and BEENE (Fred)
MATTHEW LUKE and JOHN (Tommy)

## COMING OR GOING

Three Yankees whose names are palindromes (i.e., spelled the same backward and forward).

Truck HANNAH

Toby HARRAH
Mark SALAS

## A LEAGUE OF THEIR OWN

First Base—BABE Dahlgren
Second Base—BLONDY Ryan
Shortstop—LYN Lary
Third Base—QUEENIE O'Rourke
Left Field—ANGEL Aragon
Center Field—LIZ Funk
Right Field—BABE RUTH
Catcher—BUBBLES Hargrave
Designated Hitter—HONEY Barnes
Pitcher—CUDDLES Marshall
Pitcher—LYNN McGlothen
Pitcher—ROSY Ryan

## TALE OF THE TAPE

On the morning of Friday, November 6, 2009, the city of New York celebrated the twenty-seventh World Series championship of the New York Yankees by parading the members of the team through "The Canyon of Heroes" along lower Broadway from the Battery to City Hall in a spectacular "ticker tape" parade without ticker tape.

Since the city's first ticker tape parade in 1886, through 2012, there have been 204 such parades. Not only have athletes from all sports been so honored but also heads of state, a scientist, war heroes, astronauts, a pope, and journalists have been hailed. Yet ticker tape has not been used since the 1960s when stock tickers became obsolete.

The term "ticker tape" is an anachronism that conjures up other anachronisms in baseball.

Why is a high bouncing ball to the infield called a "Baltimore Chop"?

Why do baseball players sit in a "dugout"?

Why do fans sit in the "bleachers"?

Why do pitchers warm up in the "bullpen"?

What is a "can of corn"?

It's a "Baltimore Chop" because at the turn of the twentieth century the Baltimore Orioles played on an infield so hard that a ball, when batted into the ground, would kangaroo hop to the fielders.

It's a "dugout" because benches constructed to seat players were sunk into the ground, about a foot below ground level. Today, the benches are at ground level, but it's still called a dugout and it always will be.

The "bleachers" were uncovered stands in the outfield where fans would sit, bleaching in the hot summer sun, so named because baseball fields were not equipped with lights. They're still called "bleachers" today, although most games now are played at night.

The word "bullpen," which is also prison slang for a place of temporary confinement, is of uncertain origin in baseball. Some say it can be traced to the Bull Durham tobacco signs that were posted on the fences of many ballparks in 1909. Featured on the sign was the picture of a gigantic bull, and in many parks the relief pitcher warmed up in front of the picture. As far back as 1877, however, "bullpen" was the name used for a roped-off section of the outfield that served as standing room. The term was also known to be used to describe the stockade in Civil War days.

A "can of corn" is a lazy, soft fly ball to an outfielder. Why a can of corn? History, septuagenarians, and octogenarians tell us that in the days before supermarkets, retail grocers stacked can goods on shelves that stretched to the ceiling. To procure the merchandise for a customer, the proprietor used a long-handled device that clutched the object in a vise-like grip. The proprietor would then flip the item, and from the shelf and into his hand for an easy catch would come . . . a can of corn.

What if, instead of corn, the customer ordered a can of peas? Or sauerkraut?

# NINE

# THE BOSS

Wednesday, January 3, 1973, came up clear and unseasonably mild in New York. I had awakened early, still feeling the euphoria of the Christmas holiday enjoyed with my three young children and with expectation and hope for the New Year as I prepared for the long ride from northern New Jersey across the George Washington Bridge to the Bronx and Yankee Stadium.

I had been among those summoned there by the Yankees, who were holding a "major" press conference at which they promised some "important news."

Rumors had abounded in recent days that the Yankees were about to be sold, a prospect that left me with mixed emotions. The Columbia Broadcasting System had owned the team for eight seasons and demonstrated that it was not prepared to succeed in the business of baseball as it guided (or misguided) the Yankees to one of the worst periods in the team's long and glorious history. In eight seasons under CBS aegis, the Yankees posted a winning record four times and finished sixth, tenth, ninth, and fifth in a ten-team league and fifth, second, fourth, and fourth in a six-team division.

On the other hand, I had grown fond of the man CBS put in charge of running the team. Michael Burke was charming, engaging, and flamboyant. A Renaissance man, his clothes were of the latest cut and his long gray hair was styled in the fashion of the day. He had been a star halfback on the University of Pennsylvania football team; served in World War II with General "Wild Bill" Donovan's OSS (Office of Strategic Services), predecessor of the CIA; and was awarded the Silver Star for gallantry and the Navy Cross for heroism. But he admitted to knowing little about baseball and even less about running a baseball team.

Nevertheless, I held out hope that whoever took over the team would see fit to retain Burke in some capacity.

I arrived at the Stadium and joined the horde of reporters, both print and electronic, with their television cameras and newspaper photographers in tow. There wasn't even so much as a hint as to the nature of the announcement, and if the rumors of a sale of the Yankees were true, there was not even a guess as to the name of the purchaser. If anything, any new owner of baseball's most prestigious team figured to be someone in the baseball community and/or a New Yorker of prominence.

Instead, we were surprised when it was announced that CBS had sold the Yankees for $10 million, $3.2 million less than it had paid for the team nine years before, to a 12-man group headed by George M. Steinbrenner III, of Lorain, Ohio, a suburb of Cleveland.

Who?

That was the reaction of the assembled media. Shock! Surprise! Incredulity!

Only one member of the gathered media even knew who George M. Steinbrenner III was. Bill Mazer, a popular radio sports talk show host at the time when radio sports talk shows were rare, had known Steinbrenner during Mazer's tenure as a sportscaster in Buffalo, New York. Steinbrenner was chairman of the American Shipbuilding Company in Lorain and his ship business often took him to Buffalo and other cities along the Great Lakes.

Mazer remembered that Steinbrenner had a sports background of sorts. He had been a varsity hurdler first at Culver Academy and then at Williams College and an assistant football coach at two Big Ten football powers, Northwestern and Purdue. Later he owned the Cleveland Pipers of the American Basketball League and a small piece of the Chicago Bulls, so his interest in ownership of the Yankees was a natural progression, unlike that of his predecessors CBS, Dan Topping (heir to a tin industry fortune), Del Webb (a wealthy real estate developer), and Colonel Jacob Ruppert, who purchased the Yankees to promote the sale of his Ruppert Beer.

Steinbrenner had no such ulterior motive. He sincerely desired the opportunity to own a major league franchise, and he had missed out on a chance to own his hometown team, the Cleveland Indians. He recognized that in the Yankees, he was getting the cream of the crop in Major League Baseball, perhaps in all of professional sports.

"Owning the Yankees," he famously said, "is like owning the *Mona Lisa*. It's the best buy in sports today. I think it's a bargain."

In his first address as the Yankees' principal owner, Steinbrenner said, "We plan on absentee ownership. We're not going to pretend we're something we aren't. I'll stick to building ships. I won't be active in the day-to-day operations of the ballclub at all. I can't spread myself so thin. I've got enough headaches with my shipping company."

It wasn't long before Steinbrenner's irresistible obsession with being a hands-on owner overwhelmed him. In his first spring training as Yankees owner he was seen jotting down the uniform numbers of any Yankee whose hair crept down from the back of his cap and onto his neck. He made a list of the numbers of those players who he believed were unkempt or sloppy in their dress. He reported one player for wearing his cap with the bill in the back and ordered that the player be reprimanded and punished.

"George," he was told. "He's a catcher."

It seemed inevitable that Steinbrenner and Burke would clash over control of the team, and it happened in the first months of their partnership. In the 1973 Yankees press guide, Steinbrenner and Burke are listed jointly as general partners, and Burke has the added title of chief executive officer. By April, Burke had submitted his resignation from the Yankees and took over as president of Madison Square Garden.

In his first season at the Yankees' helm, Steinbrenner decided to join the team when they played the Rangers in Texas. In an effort to fight the boredom of a long and tedious season, major league baseball players sometimes have a tendency to behave like little boys. Many enjoy playing practical jokes on unsuspecting teammates. Among the favorite foils for members of the 1973 Yankees was shortstop Gene (Stick) Michael, who had a morbid fear of things that squiggle, crawl, and go bump in the night.

"We were playing the Rangers in Texas," Michael recalled, "and Steinbrenner was there, sitting in a box seat next to our dugout. While we were batting, somebody had put half of a frankfurter in one of the fingers of my glove. When our inning was over somebody gave me my glove and I went out to shortstop. I put the glove on and I felt something slimy in there. I shook my hand and nothing came out. Then I shook my glove and a piece of a hot dog came out. So I took the hot dog and fired it toward the dugout, but it slid over in front of a security cop who was sitting on a wooden chair right in front of George, who was sitting there.

"I'll never forget this. Graig Nettles made this up, I know, but he said to me that George said, 'Give me that hot dog. I want that hot dog.' And Nettles told me that he said to George, 'What are you going to do, fingerprint it?'

"It's blurry in my mind now, but I think I remember George saying he was going to find out who put the hot dog in there and he was going to punish him. Or he told [manager Ralph] Houk to find out who did it, but Houk just ignored him."

At first Steinbrenner's appearances at Yankee Stadium were rare occasions, but as time went on he began showing up more and more—so much for "absentee ownership" and not being active in the day-to-day operation of the ball club.

When Yankee Stadium reopened in 1976 after undergoing renovations, Steinbrenner spent more time in his brand-new spacious office with its leather chairs shaped like baseball gloves and the sign that read: "Rule No. 1—The boss is always right. Rule No. 2—If the boss is wrong, see Rule No. 1."

It was just about that time that sports cartoonists and columnists began referring to Steinbrenner sardonically as "the Boss," an appellation that took hold and stayed with him until his death and that he obviously appreciated and enjoyed.

I had quickly fallen into a comfortable and cordial relationship with Steinbrenner. I discovered I could needle him and he would needle right back. I found him dynamic, personable, determined to return the Yankees to their former glory days, and a wonderful source of information about the team I was covering.

He flattered me by inviting me to his sixtieth birthday party at the Westchester home of his close friend, Bill Fugazy, and by having his secretary send a gift when he learned of the birth of my fourth child. He would call me from time to time with some inside tidbit about his team or to pick my brain. When the Yankees won the 1977 World Series, Steinbrenner said he was considering giving the team's regular beat writers World Series rings. I told him I thought that was a generous and thoughtful gesture, but that I would not accept such a gift.

"Why not?" he asked. He sounded wounded at what he probably perceived as a lack of gratitude.

"Because the Mets did that when they won the World Series in 1969," I explained. "All the writers that traveled with the team got rings and they wore them constantly and I noticed that the players resented it. Those writers didn't do anything to win the World Series and neither did we."

The rings were never presented.

From time to time, Steinbrenner would call with some nugget, a grief he wanted to get off his chest or to troll my waters for scuttlebutt. It was always the same. My phone would ring at home or in my office. I'd pick it up, and all I would hear on the other end were two words:

"It's George."

Not "Hello, how are you?" No pleasantries. No last name. Simply "It's George."

George Who? Washington? Brett? Burns? Bush? Marshall? Carlin? Clooney?

Simply "It's George," and that could mean only one thing: George M. Steinbrenner, principal owner of the New York Yankees was on the phone, returning my call or calling unsolicited because he had something on his mind, usually a complaint about one of his players, or his manager, or his pitching coach, and he wanted—needed—to get it off his chest or to plant a seed he knew would end up in the next day's newspaper.

I was not so naïve or egotistical to believe that Steinbrenner favored me because he liked my writing, my personality, my wit, or the way I combed my hair. No, I understood that not only was I one of the senior members covering the Yankees, but also I was working for the *New York Daily News*, the paper with the largest daily circulation in the nation.

Of course, I still had my disagreements with "the Boss." While I admit to supporting him on most issues, there were times when I believed his behavior to be indefensible and it was necessary to criticize him in print. On those occasions, he would react predictably. The telephone calls would stop. The tidbits of information would be directed elsewhere.

I have often said that those periods of noncommunication reminded me of going to a bakery or a deli and taking a number to await your turn to be served. Cross Steinbrenner, and he would put your number on the bottom of the pile so you would have to patiently bide your time until sooner or later all those numbers on his pile that were placed ahead of yours would in some way alienate him, your number would come back up to the top of the pile and you'd be back in his good graces once more.

After I left the *Daily News*, I would occasionally run into Steinbrenner, and always he was affable and friendly. He'd greet me warmly or sarcastically, which I knew to be his way of displaying camaraderie.

But curiously the phone calls stopped coming.

Another lesson learned from the *Boss*!

# TEN

# BILLYBALL

From Oakland, you take Route 17 North past factory smokestacks spewing their pollution into the clean summer air. Turn off at University Avenue and soon you're in West Berkeley, an old and antiseptic town with row upon row of wooden, Victorian, one-family houses. Many are boarded up with "No Trespassing" signs on their doors, waiting for the wrecker's ball to come and do their damage. Take a left turn on Seventh Street and halfway up the block you come to a small, unpretentious frame house. The address is 1632.

"This is the house I was born in," says Billy Martin. "It used to be on Sixth Street, but my mom had it moved around the corner. They put the whole house on rollers and moved it. The chimney fell off as the house was going around the block."

Billy Martin has come back home. It's August 30, 1976, and the American League schedule has the Yankees—the first-place Yankees, Billy Martin's first-place Yankees—playing a three-game series against the Athletics in nearby Oakland, which has given Martin the opportunity to visit his mother, who was still living in the same house in which she raised her son the baseball manager. On his left hand he wears a cast to protect and help heal a broken thumb. He says he broke the thumb when he was hit by a line drive in batting practice, but Billy being Billy, he is haunted by his past. Most people don't believe him.

"What did you do, Bill, punch somebody?" asks his mother upon greeting her boy.

Her name now is Mrs. Joan Downey, and she is unmistakably her son's mother, small and slim, outspoken and frank.

"He was a good boy, my Billy," she says. "When I told my kids to come home, they came home. They never stayed out late. I never had any trouble with my kids. Once they accused Billy of stealing and I told them to come on in and see me if they can find what he stole. My Billy didn't steal nothing. All that talk, all them stories that he was a mean kid when he was small, that he was a fighter. That's all bullsh . . ."

It was here that Billy Martin spent his early life, and he moves around the house easily, stopping to look at little mementoes from his childhood. "A lot of memories," he says softly, almost wistfully.

He walks up a short flight of stairs and has to duck his head to get through a door. "This was my room," he says. "I was born right here in this room. They had to put lights in so I could be born."

Martin was poor as a boy. He could never remember a time when he didn't work at some small job, as equipment manager at the local playground; as a stock boy at Cutter's Laboratories, a Berkeley pharmaceutical company; for the post office; and as a packer for Heinz 57 Varieties.

Although there was no money for luxuries, Martin never felt deprived. There always was food and clothing and loads of love from a house dominated by women—his mother and grandmother and his sisters—and there was always time for fun, to pursue what would be a lifelong passion for fishing and to go to the local wharf and catch ducks.

"I learned how to sneak up behind the ducks and catch them before they flew off," Martin recalled. "I'd take them home and we'd clean them and eat them. They were a little greasy but they tasted good."

His mother was married first to a man named Pesani and then to Billy's father, a Portuguese named Martin who skipped out on his family while Billy's mother was pregnant. When Billy was eight months old, his mother married Jack Downey.

"When I talk about my dad, that's who I mean," he said. "He was always a hardworking man, a good man. I never even saw my real father until I was in junior high school."

His mother's maiden name was Salvini, and it was Grandma Salvini, his mother's mother—an old Italian-born woman who spoke no English and helped raise Billy with equal parts of discipline and love—who had the strongest influence on a young Billy. He was at birth Alfred Manuel Martin, but it was Grandma Salvini who is responsible for the name "Billy."

"She used to call me 'bellis,' which is short for 'bellisimo,' the Italian word for beautiful. I guess all the kids heard her and thought she was saying 'Billy' and that's what they called me. I never knew my name was Alfred until my first day in junior high school. That night I told my mom that some crazy teacher was saying my name is Alfred and mom said 'It is,' and that's how I learned my real name wasn't Billy."

You had to be tough in those days to get by in West Berkeley, and Billy learned to fight at an early age in order to defend himself from older bullies and toughs. "I once had a fight that lasted over an hour," he boasted. He also recalled doing mischievous things, kid stuff, but he never got in any serious trouble. About the most serious thing he remembered doing when he was a kid was stealing a loaf of bread from a local bakery.

"Every night the bakery would put out the freshly baked loaves of bread, and we'd smell the bread and steal a loaf. We never hurt the guy, and we never stole more than a loaf. I think the owner knew we were doing it, and he never said anything because we didn't steal a lot. I believe it was his way of making sure we didn't go hungry."

What Martin remembered most from his youth was playing baseball in James Kenny Park, which was the center of his young life. He had been bitten by the baseball bug at an early age and decided he wanted to be a professional ballplayer, an ambition fostered by the fact that northern California was fertile ground for baseball players, from Chick Hafey to Lefty O'Doul to the DiMaggio brothers to Jackie Jensen.

In Martin's own neighborhood there resided a major league player, Augie Galan, who played 16 major league seasons in the 1930s and '40s, mostly with the Chicago Cubs and Brooklyn Dodgers. He would post a lifetime batting average of .287, become the first switch-hitter in baseball history to hit home runs from each side of the plate in the same game and in 1935 go to bat 649 times without hitting into a double play. And he would become a mentor and role model for young Billy Martin.

"I made up my mind when I was in high school that I was going to be a ballplayer," Martin said. "The school counselor asked me what I wanted to be, and I told her I wanted to be a professional baseball player."

It seemed a remote dream at the time. When a scout came to check out the Berkeley High School baseball team, Billy Martin was the cleanup batter and the team's leading hitter and its shortstop, yet the scout passed on him and signed another player.

One day Billy was playing in the playground and Eddie Leishman, the general manager of the Oakland Oaks of the Pacific Coast League, came looking for him. "Some kid got hurt at our Idaho Falls farm team," Leishman said. "We need a replacement. I'll give you two hundred dollars a month and a three-hundred-dollar signing bonus."

Martin would have jumped at the chance for nothing, but he used part of the $300 bonus to buy a suitcase and a pair of slacks. "I didn't even have a glove," Martin said. "I took one from the equipment room at the playground and used it all season, then returned it when I came home. At Idaho Falls they put me right in the lineup at third base. The first ball that was hit to me, there was a man on first and I picked up the ball and threw to second to start a double play. The ball was foul. I knew it but I threw to second any way. The umpire never knew the ball was foul."

Back in Yankee Stadium, the walls of Martin's manager's office are bare except for one solitary picture, the familiar craggy face of Casey Stengel. On the left sleeve of his Yankees uniform, Martin wore a black arm band, a memoriam to Stengel, recently departed. It is said that on the night Stengel passed, Martin gained entry to Casey's house and slept in his bed.

"I loved that old man," Martin said. "I loved him like a father. I don't know what I might have been doing today if it were not for him."

Stengel was already old, a broken down ex-ballplayer, twice a failure as a major league manager, but he was the manager of the Oakland Oaks when Martin got there in 1948.

"He'd hit me groundballs before the game," Martin remembered. "He'd hit them by the hour, and one day I heard him tell somebody, 'That big-nose kid is not the smoothest fielder I ever saw, but he never gets tired.'" Martin considered it one of the nicest things anybody ever said about him.

A year later Stengel became the manager of the New York Yankees, and a year after that, the Yankees purchased Martin's contract from the Oakland Oaks. Martin was convinced it was Stengel's doing. He joined the Yankees in the spring of 1950.

"I was awed in spring training, surrounded by all those stars [Yogi Berra, Phil Rizzuto, Tommy Henrich, Hank Bauer, Johnny Mize, Vic Raschi, Allie Reynolds, Eddie Lopat, and the great Joe DiMaggio, who had just won the World Series]. They gave me a hard time because I had a reputation that I was brash. But I was really shy. I felt lost so far from home. I think Joe DiMaggio realized, or maybe because we were both Italians and were both from the same area in northern California. One day he invited me to have dinner with him, and the next thing I knew I was palling around with him. Me, a rookie, hanging out with the greatest player in the game! The other players got on me about it, and I told them the reason DiMag chose me to hang with was that I had class."

Martin made his major league debut on April 18, 1950, opening day in Boston, entering the game in the sixth inning as a defensive replacement at second base for Jerry Coleman. In a typical Fenway Park slugfest, the Yankees trailed 10–4 in the eighth inning when they scored nine runs. In his first major league at-bat in the inning, Martin doubled in Yogi Berra. Later in the inning, Martin batted again and singled in two runs. The Yankees went on to win the game, 15–10.

A month later Martin had only three more official at-bats before he was sent back to Kansas City.

"Aint ya mad?" Stengel asked him.

"Yeah, I'm mad," Martin said.

"Well then, why dontcha go up there and tell [George] Weiss [the Yankees' general manager] off?"

"I think the old man wanted me to tell Weiss off because he was feuding with him, and that's what I did," Martin said. "I don't think Weiss ever forgot that. The first chance he got to get rid of me he did."

Weiss's chance came seven years later, after Martin had helped the Yankees win five pennants and four World Series, had batted .333 in those five World Series, had saved the 1952 Series with the now classic catch of Jackie Robinson's windblown pop fly, had batted .500, collected 12 hits, and knocked in 8 runs in the 1953 World Series, and after the famed Copacabana Incident.

"It was my birthday and a bunch of the guys wanted to help me celebrate," Martin said. "We went to dinner and then to the Copacabana night club to see Sammy Davis, Jr. They put us at a table in the back of the room and we were having a good time, enjoying the show when all of a sudden Hank Bauer nudges me and says, 'See those five guys over there? They're looking for trouble. One of those guys is giving me a bad time.'

"We went outside and one of the guys came over to me and I'm thinking this is trouble, but instead the guy said, 'Look, my brother and your friend [Bauer] have been going at it all night. We have to keep them apart.'

"I said that was fine with me, and the next thing I knew there was a crash and Hank was going at it with the guy's brother and all hell had broken loose. The newspapers found out about it and naturally I got the blame, and thirty days later Weiss traded me."

After a twenty-year exile from the Yankees as a player with Kansas City, Detroit, Cleveland, Cincinnati, Milwaukee, and

Minnesota; a coach with the Twins, a minor league manager; and a major league manager with the Minnesota Twins, Detroit Tigers, and Texas Rangers, Martin returned to his first love, the Yankees. He came with the reputation of being baseball's Mr. Fixit, a wizard at turning losing teams into winners. At the same time, his reputation was that wherever he went, he quickly wore out his welcome. The pattern was always the same. He would be called upon as a savior for a floundering franchise, improve the team immediately, but ultimately, and in a very short period of time, he would become embroiled in some off-the-field controversy or some dispute with his owner or his general manager and he would be asked to leave.

In Minnesota he led the Twins to their first championship in four years. He took a team that had a record of 79–83 and finished in seventh place and won the American League West with a mark of 97–65. He was fired that winter.

"My problem in Minnesota was the team's traveling secretary," he insisted. "The guy never wanted me to be the manager in the first place. He had the owner's ear and he kept undermining me, and he finally got me fired." (Not mentioned by Billy was a little thing about him punching out of Twins pitcher Dave Boswell outside a Detroit watering hole.)

In Detroit, where the Tigers hadn't won a thing since 1968, he took over a fourth-place 79–83 team and finished second in 1971 with a record of 91–71 and third in 1972 with a record of 86–70. He was fired with 26 games remaining in the 1973 season. Without him, the Tigers dropped into last place over the next two years.

"Everything seemed real great in Detroit," Martin alleged. "Mr. Fetzer [Tigers' owner John Fetzer] was very friendly to me, but it seemed the friendlier he got, the more Jim Campbell [the Tigers' general manager] disliked me. It was Campbell who fired me, and I think it was just a case of jealousy, that's all."

In Texas he took over a team that would finish sixth with a record of 57–105, climbing aboard for the final 23 games of the season. The next year he brought his team home in second place in the AL West with a record of 84–76 and helped the Rangers draw one million fans at home for the first time. A year later he was fired after 95 games.

"I was hired to manage the Rangers by the owner, Bob Short, who I knew from my days in Minnesota where he was a big, influential politician [Bob Short served for a time as chairman of the National Democratic Party]," Martin explained. "I'd probably have stayed there for the rest of my career if he didn't sell the team. I had an understanding with Bob that I would be involved with all the personnel decisions. The new owner wanted recognition. He told somebody when he took over the team that his goal was to fire me and get rid of the commissioner [Bowie Kuhn] by the All-Star game. He made good on half of his promises.

"In every case, I was the one who was blamed. They fired me and went around bad-mouthing me. Well, I didn't fire Billy Martin; somebody else did."

In New York, he came aboard with 56 games remaining for a team that would finish 83–77, and in his first full season as manager he would deliver a record of 97–62 then route to the Yankees' first pennant in twelve years. In the World Series, the Yankees were blitzed by the Cincinnati Reds, Sparky Anderson's "Big Red Machine," in a four-game sweep. Martin, who never took losing gracefully, rued the sweep. He was embarrassed by it. So was George Steinbrenner, who lay the blame on Martin's doorstep and ordered him to do better next year, or else.

Thus challenged, Martin drove his team to 100 wins the following year and a World Series victory in six games over the Los Angeles Dodgers. It was the Yankees' first World Series championship in fifteen years. Martin was riding high. He was the king of New York.

As usual, it didn't last. Not even for a year. A confrontation in the Fenway Park dugout with Reggie, followed by an ill-advised, alcohol-influenced comment about Jackson and Steinbrenner in Chicago's O'Hare Airport, and the next time Martin was seen in public, he was tearfully announcing his "resignation" as manager of the Yankees. That, too, would not last. Several days later, at the Yankees' annual Old Timers Day celebration, the public address announcer, Bob Sheppard, was telling a Yankee Stadium crowd of 46,711, "[T]he Yankees will like to announce at this time . . . introduce and announce at the same moment, that the manager of the 1980 season, and hopefully many years after that, will be Number One, Billy Martin."

The capacity crowd went wild with excitement as a vindicated Martin sprinted onto the field.

In the years that followed, Martin and Steinbrenner would be portrayed as baseball's version of Elizabeth Taylor and Richard Burton: they couldn't live together and they couldn't live apart. When they were apart, they lusted after one another; when they were together, they fought like a Hatfield and a McCoy.

Taylor and Burton married and divorced twice.

Martin and Steinbrenner outdid them.

Steinbrenner hired Martin on August 2, 1975, twelve days after he was fired by the Texas Rangers. Martin "resigned" on July 24, 1978, the day after Billy's "One's a born liar, the other's convicted" remark. Five days later, Steinbrenner's regret surfaced, and the Yankees announced that Martin would return as manager in 1980. But Steinbrenner couldn't wait to bring Martin back. On June 18, 1979, with the Yankees limping along at 34–31, in fourth place and eight games out of first, Steinbrenner jumped the gun and reached out for "Quick Fix" Billy Martin.

On October 23, 1979, Martin was accused of punching out a marshmallow salesman in a Minnesota hotel bar. Five days later Steinbrenner called a press conference to announce that Martin was being relieved of his managing duties and would be replaced by his third base coach, Dick Howser.

Martin, who once boasted that if Steinbrenner fired him, "I'll come back and beat him with another team," was hired by quirky Oakland Athletics owner Charles O. Finley to manage his team. Employing an exciting brand of baseball that Oakland writers dubbed "BillyBall," Martin extended his quick-fix magic to the West Coast and led the Athletics to first place in the American League West. However, he failed to live up to his prediction when the Yankees scored a three-game sweep of Oakland in the American League Championship Series.

On October 20, 1982, Finley fired Martin, and Steinbrenner waited (impatiently, no doubt) all of eighty-four days before bringing his favorite dance partner/whipping boy back as manager. Billy Martin III replaced a triumvirate of managers—Bob Lemon, who was followed by Gene Michael, who was followed by Clyde King.

It wasn't long before Liz and Dick, er, George and Billy, began sniping at one another. As usual, Steinbrenner had the last word, and Martin was fired on December 10, 1983, and replaced by Yogi Berra. But Martin would not be out of work, or out of Steinbrenner's thoughts, very long. Berra won 87 games, four fewer than Martin had won the previous season, and he finished in third place, just as Martin had. Berra had one fatal flaw in Steinbrenner's view. He wasn't Billy. Steinbrenner had said that Berra would be his manager for the entire 1984 season "no matter what." But a Boss—make that *the* Boss—has a right to change his mind, doesn't he? Steinbrenner changed his mind. After sixteen games, Berra was out and you-know-who was in.

Yet it soon became apparent during the 1985 season, even to Steinbrenner, that the Martin Magic was gone. Some things never change. On September 20, Martin got into it with one of his pitchers, Ed Whitson. It started in the bar of the hotel the team was staying at in suburban Baltimore, and it reached its climax in the courtyard just outside the bar. Martin ended up with a broken right arm and a pink slip (he now had a collection of four pink slips from Steinbrenner). On October 27, Martin was fired and replaced by Lou Piniella, and we had seen the last of Billy Martin as manager of the Yankees. Or had we?

We would come to learn that Billy Martin never would be too far from Steinbrenner's thoughts or the Yankees manager's office. On August 10, 1986, the Yankees staged "Billy Martin Day" at Yankee Stadium, and Martin's uniform No. 1 was retired, all of it undoubtedly choreographed by Steinbrenner, who presumably made Martin a promise. That promise came to fruition on October 19, 1987. Lou Piniella had just completed his second season as manager of the Yankees. He had won 179 games in the two years, an excellent winning percentage, but he had finished in second and fourth place, respectively, and that was unacceptable.

Fifteen days after their final game of the season, the Yankees announced that Piniella would not return as manager in 1988. The new (old) manager would be (you guessed it) Billy Martin.

The 1988 baseball season proved the old adage that the more things change the more they stay the same. Revitalized and refreshed, the Martin Magic returned, and he got the Yankees off to a flying start. They won their first five games and nine of their first ten. By May 6, the Yankees had won 20 of 28 games and were in first place by 2½ games. They also were on Martin's home turf,

Arlington, Texas, where he had many friends and knew all the hot spots. After a night game, he caught up with his old buddy, and best friend, Mickey Mantle, and off they went with a few others to a topless club called Lace.

The exact details of what went on in the club have never been made public. What we do know is that Martin got into some sort of dispute and ended up being pummeled by the club's bouncers. Ordinarily, Steinbrenner would have fired Martin on the spot, but the team was off to such a hot start, and the Boss let Martin off with just a warning.

But when the team cooled off—as inevitably it figured to—losing four straight and seven out of eight and going from two games up to 2½ games behind, Steinbrenner dropped the other shoe. He fired Martin and replaced him with the manager Martin had replaced, Lou Piniella.

Move over Liz and Dick. The count, if you're keeping score, was now five hirings and five firings of Martin by Steinbrenner. Sadly, there would be no Billy VI.

I am not unmindful of Billy Martin's foibles. I am fully cognizant of his flaws. For the most part I disapproved of his frequent boorish behavior, and I make no attempt to defend, excuse, or explain that behavior.

I believe there were two Billy Martins. There was the fiery, feisty, combative Billy Martin, sometimes meanspirited, always fiercely competitive. The only thing he ever wanted was to manage his beloved New York Yankees.

And there was another Billy Martin, a warm, outgoing, generous, compassionate Billy Martin, courteous with fans, giving of his time to those in need, affectionate with children. He loved kids. He loved his church. He loved his family. And he loved the Yankees.

That's the Billy Martin that few have seen. I am pleased, and privileged, to have been one of those few.

After he was fired by George Steinbrenner for the fifth time, Martin retired to his horse farm in Port Crane, New York, just outside Binghamton, believing in his heart that at some point Steinbrenner would grow disenchanted with his current manager, no matter who it was, and that he would once again obsess over Billy Martin and there would be a Billy VI with the Yankees.

In the summer of 1989, I had planned a trip to upstate New York with my fourteen-year-old son, John. We would visit the Baseball Hall of Fame and Museum at Cooperstown and then take a tour of minor league baseball in New York State. I had called Martin and told him about my trip and asked if he might be receptive to a visit from me and my son. He said we would be more than welcome. In fact, he seemed eager about it.

We arrived at the Martin farm shortly after noon. Billy had arranged for a local college student to keep my son amused and entertained by taking him fishing on a lake on Martin's property while he and I talked. Billy looked rested and relaxed, healthier than I had seen him in years. He seemed to enjoy the role of country squire. But as we talked I found him in a rare nostalgic and contemplative mood, reflecting on his past and coming to grips, somewhat regretfully, with his own idiosyncrasies. It also became apparent that he was convinced he would one day get a call from Steinbrenner and he would be putting on his old uniform No. 1 and occupying the manager's office in Yankee Stadium once more.

When my son John returned from his fishing expedition brandishing a one-pound largemouth bass, his catch, Martin asked him if he liked spaghetti. When John said he did, Martin set about preparing a spaghetti dinner, boiling the water, cooking the spaghetti, and making the sauce himself.

After dinner, Martin and I said our goodbyes and I headed home with my son, fully expecting that the next time I saw Martin he would be managing the Yankees once more.

I never saw him again.

Four months after my visit to Martin's farm, I was at sea, on a Christmas Caribbean cruise with members of my family when I received a phone call informing me that Martin had been killed on Christmas Day in a car crash near his property in Port Crane. I was asked if I could be available to serve as a pall bearer at the funeral in St. Patrick's Cathedral two days later. I had to decline the invitation because there was no way I could leave my young son and daughter on the cruise.

Not being able to attend the funeral of Billy Martin remains to this day my forever regret.

# ELEVEN

# REGGIE'S PANTS

The dynamics around the Yankees changed dramatically the moment Reginald Martinez Jackson put on the pinstripes for the first time. From then on, things would never be the same in the Bronx and neither would the Yankees.

Reggie Jackson and the Yankees was a union ordained by fate, and by time, Jackson's availability colliding with the emancipation of baseball players through free agency; free agency colliding with George M. Steinbrenner's purchase of sport's most prestigious franchise from the Columbia Broadcasting System; Steinbrenner's ownership colliding with his willingness and his ability to open his checkbook and throw huge, obscene wads of cash at the game's biggest stars, of which at the time there was none bigger than Jackson.

"Go get the big man," Thurman Munson urged Steinbrenner. "He's the only guy in baseball that can carry a club for a month. The hell with what you hear. He hustles every minute on the field."

And Steinbrenner listened to his catcher. He went and he got the "big man."

"He hustled me like a broad," Jackson said of Steinbrenner. "George can sell sand to the Arabs."

Steinbrenner's lust was hardly unrequited. Just who was the hustler here and who was the hustlee?

Almost two years before free agency came to baseball Jackson had already begun targeting the Yankees. He openly and brazenly campaigned to make New York his future home. He watched his Oakland A's teammate Catfish Hunter gain his freedom and sign a lucrative contract and he, too, wanted out of Oakland to escape the penny-pinching ownership of Charles O. Finley.

With Jackson as their marquee player—and the American League's premier power hitter who had led the league in home runs in two of the three previous seasons—the A's had won consecutive World Series championships in 1972, '73, and '74. Now they were on the verge of becoming the first to win four consecutive World Series since the New York Yankees completed a run of five in a row twenty-two years before.

To reach their goal, the A's first had to defeat the Boston Red Sox in a five-game 1975 American League Championship Series scheduled to start in Boston's historic Fenway Park on Saturday, October 4.

The day before, the two teams worked out in Fenway, first the visiting A's and then the home team Red Sox. His workout concluded, Jackson, still in his Oakland gold and gray uniform, found a seat in the stands down the left field line and watched the Red Sox go through their paces, knowing full well that a crowd of baseball writers would soon flock to him like flies to a garbage dump.

Jackson was almost always affable with the press and usually accessible. He considered himself a thinking man's ballplayer, an intelligent man who liked to display his extensive vocabulary with these men of words.

Not only was Jackson the key man for the three-time defending World Series champions, and therefore a prominent figure in the upcoming ALCS, but also he was an important news story, the most attractive and most desirable of the potential free agents who had made it known he no longer wanted to play in Oakland for Finley and that he would look to go elsewhere if and when he was able to attain free agency status.

There were frequent reports that Jackson's desire was to play in New York, the cultural and media capital of the world where endorsements and the opportunity to supplement one's income would be plentiful. The reports said that he wanted to play for the Yankees, who had the history and tradition that an aware Jackson greatly admired, and for George Steinbrenner, an owner who had made it clear he would pay top dollar for talent.

With all this in mind, someone asked Jackson, seated along the left field line in Fenway Park, how he felt about one day playing for the Yankees. He paused momentarily and then, staring pointedly at those in the crowd he knew to be employed by New York newspapers, he replied: "If I played in New York, they'd name a candy bar after me."

It was a revealing comment, supposedly delivered spontaneously, and yet it came across as carefully thought out, studied, and rehearsed for delivery at the propitious moment, and fraught with innuendo.

It spoke of Jackson's desire to play in New York. It served notice to Steinbrenner—certain to hear of Reggie's comment—that he wanted to be a Yankee (while Major League Baseball had a tampering rule against any owner or team representative that expressed a desire to covet a player employed by another team, there was no such rule against a player employed by one team expressing a desire to play for another team). And it told of Jackson's knowledge of history, for legend had it that the Baby Ruth candy bar was named for the redoubtable Babe Ruth. Reggie was clearly implying that playing in New York, for the Yankees, he would be as big a star as Ruth, big enough to, like the mighty Babe, have a candy bar named after him. (Eventually, Wayne Candies did produce a "Reggie Bar." It was similar to the Baby Ruth, peanuts and caramel dipped in chocolate, but it was not a "bar," like the Baby Ruth. Instead it was shaped like a baseball, round, but flat. It debuted in 1978 and was gone within a few years except for a brief but short-lived revival in 1993, the year Jackson was elected to the Hall of Fame.)

It did not matter that the legend of the Baby Ruth being named for Babe Ruth never was authenticated. The bar was produced by the Chicago-based Curtis Candy Company, which steadfastly maintained that it was named not for the baseball player but for Ruth Cleveland, the young daughter of President Grover Cleveland. The fact that the bar first hit the market in 1921, at the peak of Babe Ruth's success and popularity, thirty years after Cleveland left office and seventeen years after Ruth Cleveland passed away suggests that the Curtis Company may have concocted the story to avoid having to pay royalties to the Yankees' Ruth and his estate.

For Jackson, it didn't matter how or why the Baby Ruth bar got its name. He had made his point and trotted out his advertising slogan.

"That was typical Reggie," said Matt Merola, Jackson's longtime New York–based business agent. "He said it. Nobody prompted him. It was not something that we ever discussed before. It was entirely spontaneous; Reggie being Reggie. It was a beautiful line because it said so much in so little."

Jackson—"I didn't come to New York to become a star; I brought my star with me"—swept into Yankeeland all bluster, braggadocio, and bravado. He came, he saw, and he confounded. He would be the most polarizing player in Yankees history (only two years old at the time, Alex Rodriguez would not arrive for three decades). In short order Jackson would clash with the owner, defy the manager, and disrespect the team's best player, who had been his biggest booster.

Jackson had been in camp a little more than a week when he sat down in a Fort Lauderdale watering hole for a lengthy, far-ranging interview with a writer from *Sport Magazine*. The article would not be seen until advanced copies of the magazine circulated around the Yankees' clubhouse in the seventh week of the season, on May 19, and it would rock the mighty and proud franchise to its foundation.

The article was typical Reggie—self-serving, boastful, defiant, and egocentric. Worst of all it picked for its target and demeaned the most respected, admired, and beloved Yankee, Thurman Munson.

"This team, it all flows from me," Jackson is quoted in the article. "I've got to keep it going. I'm the straw that stirs the drink. It all comes back to me. Maybe I should say me and Munson. But really he doesn't enter into it. He's so damned insecure. Munson thinks he can be the straw that stirs the drink, but he can only stir it bad."

Munson was understandably stunned by Jackson's words. His teammates, who had seen him rise up the ranks in the Yankees farm system and had earned his stripes with his leadership and excellent play over eight seasons and who considered him the heart and soul of the team, rallied around their captain and friend.

Jackson's defense was that he was misquoted.

"For four pages?" asked Munson, who would refuse to shake Jackson's hand after a home run.

The article was a torpedo in the turbulent sea that was the Yankees clubhouse and caused a chasm therein, with players choosing sides. The large majority lined up with Munson, the veteran Yankee, against Jackson, the interloper. For manager Billy Martin, the choice was a no-brainer. He had made his choice weeks earlier.

Martin never wanted Jackson. He urged Steinbrenner to sign Reggie's teammate, Joe Rudi, because "he's a better player than Jackson."

Steinbrenner refused to accede to Martin's wishes, and Billy had no choice but to accept Jackson. But he didn't have to like it. To demonstrate his displeasure with Steinbrenner's choice, Martin seemed to go out of his way to humiliate Jackson (at least Reggie thought so). He wrote Jackson's name on his list of players assigned to take every road trip in spring training. (Veteran players usually are allowed to miss most road trips during the exhibition season and play mostly home games; when Jackson complained to some writers that Martin was penalizing him by having him make every trip and the writers took Reggie's complaint to the manager, Martin said, "He asked me to let him make every trip.") In addition, Martin refused to bat Jackson third or fourth in the batting order, as Steinbrenner suggested and Jackson expected (Munson was his No. 3 hitter and Chris Chambliss his No. 4 hitter; Jackson batted either fifth or sixth).

The relationship between the headstrong manager and his new, self-acclaimed superstar player was an uneasy one that finally erupted into a full-scale confrontation on Saturday, June 18, 1977, in Boston's Fenway Park. All the tension, all the turmoil, all the frustration, all the festering hostility that had been building for months erupted in an ugly scene in full view of 34,603 fans and a national television audience that included George Steinbrenner watching from his home in Florida.

It was the sixth inning, and the Yankees were trailing 7–4 on their way to a third straight defeat to the hated Red Sox, when Jim Rice dropped a hit into right field in front of Jackson, who was slow retrieving the ball as Rice chugged into second base. Jackson said it was caution. Martin said it was indifference.

Soon Martin was on his way to the mound to make a pitching change. At the same time Paul Blair was on his way to right field.

"You here for me?" a quizzical Jackson asked Blair.

Blair nodded his assent.

"What the hell's going on?"

"You've got to ask Billy that," said Blair.

Perplexed, astonished, and embarrassed, Jackson trotted in from his position and ducked into the dugout. Martin was at the opposite end of the dugout but headed toward Jackson when the right fielder arrived. They had words. The veins could be seen bulging in Martin's neck as he lunged toward Jackson and was restrained in a bear hug by coach Yogi Berra. This is Jackson's version of what transpired in the dugout:

"When I got to the top step of the dugout, I could see there was fury about him [Martin], and it was all directed toward me. When Billy starts to lose it, the veins in his neck become more prominent. Now they were standing at attention.

"I started down the steps toward the other corner of the dugout from where he was. He screamed over to me. "'What the (bleep) do you think you're doing out there?'

"I put my glove down and took my glasses off. I put the glasses down on the top of my glove. Afterward, everybody read that as a sign that I was getting myself ready to fight him. I wasn't. At the time, I was just taking my glasses off, which I often do when I come off the field.

"I looked at him. 'What do you mean? What are you talking about?'

"He started down the dugout toward me.

"'You know what the (bleep) I'm talking about,' he said. 'You want to show me up by loafing on me? Fine! Then I'm going to show your ass up. Anyone who doesn't hustle doesn't play for me.'

"'I wasn't loafing, Billy,' I said. 'But I'm sure that doesn't matter to you. Nothing I could ever do would please you. You never wanted me on this team in the first place. You don't want me now. Why don't you just admit it?'

"The distance between us had shortened considerably. Elston Howard was trying to get between us. Yogi was there, and Jimmy Wynn.

"Billy was still screaming.

"'I ought to kick your (bleeping) ass' was the next thing I heard. And then I'd had enough.

"'Who the (bleep) do you think you're talking to, old man?' I snapped, just about spitting out the words.

"'What?' Billy yelled. 'Who's an old man? Who are you calling an old man?'

"I guess in Billy's mind he was still twenty-five years old and the toughest kid on the street corner. He came for me. Elston and Yogi grabbed him. Jimmy Wynn grabbed me from behind.

"'You're an old man,' I said. 'You're forty-nine years old and you weigh one hundred sixty. I'm thirty and weigh two hundred ten. Let me tell you something. You aren't going to do (bleep). What you are is plain crazy.'"

This was Martin's version:

"I didn't like the way Reggie went after the ball. I thought he dogged it, and I just can't have that sort of thing on my team. I had told my players at the beginning of the season if they embarrassed me on the field, I was going to embarrass them. I knew the other twenty-four players were looking to see how I was going to handle this, with Reggie being a superstar and having the big contract. I thought if I did what had to be done, that would bring George down on me. But if I let it pass, I would lose the other twenty-four players.

"I knew what I had to do. I told Paul Blair to go out to right field and tell Reggie he was being replaced. I meant to teach him a lesson.

"When he came into the dugout, Reggie challenged me. He kept telling me he didn't like being shown up, and I replied, 'If you show me up, I'll show you up.' Then he swore at me, and that did it, we almost came to blows. Elston Howard and Yogi Berra had to pull us apart."

Later that night, Steve Jacobson of *Newsday*, Paul Montgomery of the *New York Times*, and I went to Reggie's room. Mike Torrez, the Yankees' starting pitcher that afternoon, was there to console his friend and lend his moral support. Jackson appeared to be near a breakdown, first rational and calm and slowly becoming more passionate. He was stripped to the waist, medals and chins around his neck, dangling at his chest. Perspiration glistened on his bare chest, and soon tears began to stream down his face.

He was on his knees as if in prayer, delivering a sermon like an evangelist, pouring out anger, frustration, and anguish along with his perspiration and tears, wondering why he was being persecuted, why he was so misunderstood, unappreciated, and unwanted. The sweat and the tears formed a pool on the floor at his knees.

"It makes me cry the way they treat me on this team," he said. "I'm a big black man with an IQ of one hundred sixty, making seven hundred thousand dollars a year and they treat me like dirt. They never had anyone like me on their team before."

Steinbrenner's first impulse was to fire Martin, but team president Gabe Paul's cooler head prevailed. He made Steinbrenner see that to do so would be tantamount to handing his team over to Jackson. Steinbrenner backed off and allowed Paul to be mediator. He brokered an uneasy peace between player and manager, each making huge concessions.

On August 10, Martin installed Jackson in the cleanup position in his batting order to stay and Reggie responded by hitting 13 home runs and driving in 49 runs in the final 53 games of the regular season, and leading the Yankees to their second straight American League East championship. And for the second straight year, the Yankees engaged the Kansas City Royals in the American League Championship Series. The two heated rivals exchanged two victories each in the best-of-five series and they came down to the climactic fifth game in Kansas City.

Before the series, a confident Jackson had boasted, "We'll win because we're a team of great character."

Now, in this do-or-die fifth game, Jackson's character was being put to the supreme test. When he arrived at Royals Stadium he learned to his chagrin that his name was not in the starting lineup. How was that possible? Reggie Jackson, the ultimate big stage, clutch performer, the game changer? Reggie thought he knew the answer. It was vengeance. "Billy slapping me down one more time," he would say much later, but for now Jackson knew he had to play the role of the good soldier, and he played it through clenched teeth.

"I was surprised, shocked, hurt," he said. "You've got to be down. The season was on the line, and I was on the bench. Your pride is hurt, but I didn't want to be a problem. Not then. The writers came around looking for me to make a scene, but I wasn't going to do it. What I told them was, 'The man says I'm not playing, I'm not playing. He shouldn't be concerned about Reggie Jackson. He should manage the game.'"

According to Billy, that's precisely what he was doing, putting personal differences aside to win the game; doing what he believed was best for the team. He felt justified in his decision, pointing out that Jackson had been 1-for-14, a single with no runs batted in and that in Game 1 he had been 0-for-4 with a strikeout against Paul Splittorff, the tall, veteran left-hander who was named by Royals manager Whitey Herzog to start this fifth game.

"Reggie," Martin insisted, "can't hit Splittorff with a paddle."

So it was Paul Blair in right field for the Yankees and Cliff Johnson batting cleanup against Splittorff and the Royals took a 3–1 lead into the eighth inning.

Willie Randolph opened the inning with a single and Herzog pulled Splittorff and replaced him with right-hander Doug Bird. Thurman Munson struck out and Lou Piniella singled; two on, one out, and Cliff Johnson due up.

It was here that Martin swallowed his pride and proved his top priority was winning the game by making the move he believed necessary. He looked down the bench, caught Jackson's eye, and said, "Reggie, hit for Cliff."

And it was here that Jackson swallowed his pride and delivered in the clutch. He lashed an RBI single that cut the score to 3–2 and gave the Yankees hope for the ninth inning. They would score three times in the ninth for a 5–3 win. Jackson and Martin had both earned their justification. And the best was yet to come.

Jackson's clutch RBI single earned him his just reward, the cleanup spot in Martin's batting order in Game 1 of the World Series against the Los Angeles Dodgers.

Jackson had a harmless single in the first game, was hitless in Game 2, and had an RBI single in Game 3 as the Yankees won two of the first three games. Reggie was just getting warm. In Game 4 he led off the second inning with a double to start a three-run rally and homered in the sixth as the Yankees took a three games to one lead with a 4–2 victory.

The Dodgers kept their hopes alive by winning the fifth game despite a single by Jackson in the eighth and his second home run of the series, a solo shot in the ninth. That sent the teams back to Yankees Stadium, where the Yankees needed to win one out of two games to clinch their first World Series title in fifteen years.

Tuesday night October 18, 1977, came up cool and clear in the Bronx as a crowd of 56,407 gathered at Yankee Stadium for what they hoped was a coronation. What they got was history.

Jackson batted for the first time in the bottom of the second inning and led off with a walk. He scored on Chris Chambliss's home run.

In the fourth inning, with the Dodgers leading, 3–2, and Munson on first base, Jackson drove Burt Hooton's first pitch into the right field seats to give the Yankees a 4–3 lead.

In the fifth inning, he batted against reliever Elias Sosa with Willie Randolph on base and blasted the first pitch into the right field seats. The Yankees led, 7–3.

Jackson led off the bottom of the eighth against knuckleballer Charlie Hough. Again he swung at the first pitch and sent this one deep into the Bronx night, a monster shot into the bleachers in center field.

Three at-bats! Three pitches against three different pitchers! Three home runs! Only Babe Ruth had ever hit three home runs in a World Series game. Twice! But not on three consecutive pitches against three different pitchers. In fact, counting his home run in his final at-bat of Game 5, Jackson had hit four home runs on four consecutive pitches off four different pitchers. Babe Ruth, who may or may not have had a candy bar named after him, had never done that.

Reggie Jackson was "Mr. October," a nickname given him by, of all teammates, Thurman Munson.

As he circled the bases after his third home run, he was awash in chants of "Reggie . . . Reggie . . . Reggie . . ." from the capacity Yankee Stadium crowd.

Rounding third base and heading for home, Jackson blew kisses at the stadium's press level in the direction of the owner's box. When he had reached the dugout, waiting for him, ready to throw his arms around his cleanup hitter in a congratulatory embrace, was manager Billy Martin.

Some two hours after the final out, after the cheering had subsided and the stadium had been cleared, after the champagne had been splashed around the clubhouse, after most of the reporters, cameras, and combatants had left, Reggie Jackson was still basking in the glow of his remarkable performance. It seemed he didn't want to leave, didn't want this night to end. Still dressed in his uniform, he walked into the manager's office and plopped on a couch.

"I hit three home runs tonight, Skip" he gushed. Do you realize that? Three home runs!"

"Yeah, and you broke my record [for extra base hits in a World Series], and that tees me off."

"Billy Martin," Jackson said. "I love the man. I love Billy Martin. The man did a hell of a job this year. There's nobody I'd rather play for."

Only four months before they had stared down one another in a Fenway Park dugout and threatened to tear one another apart and now they were conducting a love fest in Yankee Stadium.

"Weak is the man who cannot accept adversity," Jackson said. "Next year we're going to be tougher, aren't we, Skip?"

"You bet we will," said Martin.

It was time to leave. Jackson strolled to his locker, and I started for home, but as I headed for the door I spotted Jackson, sitting alone at his locker, still in his uniform. I went over and offered my congratulations and told him his was the greatest one-man performance I had witnessed in covering some twenty World Series and wondered if he would favor me with some small memento of the occasion. When he graciously consented to do so, I fully expected him to peel off his wrist bands and hand them to me. Instead, he reached down, pulled off his pinstriped uniform pants, and handed them to me.

It's almost forty years later, and I still have Reggie's pants.

# TWELVE

## E-5

Just to the right as you entered the home team dressing room in Yankee Stadium—I mean the "old" Yankee Stadium, the "House that Ruth Built" Yankee Stadium—one could discover a sanctuary away from the craziness that was the "Bronx Zoo." This was the locker that housed Graig Nettles, an island of perspective, reason, and wit in a sea of lunacy.

Having arrived in the Bronx from Cleveland following the 1972 season, Nettles was at the forefront of what would become a Yankees renaissance. At the time of his arrival the Yankees were nearing the climax of what would be, except for their first eighteen years in New York, the worst drought in the team's history. They would go eleven years without finishing in first place.

By 1972, they were beginning to dig their way out of the morass. Two trades, both emphatically endorsed by their manager Ralph Houk, were being hailed as critical to the resurgence. Houk had long coveted a relief pitcher with the Boston Red Sox and a third baseman with the Cleveland Indians. The relief pitcher, Albert Walter (Sparky) Lyle came first, in a trade for veteran Danny Cater, a right-handed slugger whose power was blunted by Yankee Stadium's cavernous left field expanse but made him appealing to the Red Sox with their cozy left field "Green Monster."

Houk was slightly ahead of his time in recognizing the importance of a relief pitcher (they were not called closers in the 1970s).

"I used to believe that you built a pitching staff from the front [the starting rotation] to the back [the bullpen]," Houk said. "But I've changed, and now I believe you build a pitching staff from the back to the front."

Not only had Lyle saved 53 games and finished seventh, sixth, and third in the American League in saves the previous three seasons (at the time saves were not an official statistic of Major League Baseball and were not officially recorded, but the Elias Sports Bureau was commissioned to update and record all statistics in later years), he was a left-hander with a devastating wipeout slider that would make him a potent weapon against left-handed hitters in Yankee Stadium with its short right field porch.

In his first season as a Yankee, Lyle led the league with 35 saves, obliterating the club record (it would last for thirteen years), but the Yankees won only 79 games and finished in fourth place in the American League East for the second straight year. It was obvious there was still work to be done. There also remained lust in Houk's heart, and the Yankees assuaged that desire by pulling off a six-player trade with the Cleveland Indians, which involved sending four young players (John Ellis, Jerry Kenney, Charlie Spikes, and Rusty Torres) to Cleveland in exchange for catcher Jerry Moses and Graig Nettles.

Nettles was the player that raised Houk's heart rate. Houk liked Nettles's defense all right, but he loved his left-handed stroke that was tailor-made for Yankee Stadium. (It didn't hurt that Nettles reminded Houk of another left-handed pull hitter named Roger Maris, who had also played for the Indians before coming to the Yankees. Could it have been mere happenstance that the Yankees assigned Maris's old uniform No. 9 to Nettles?)

After Clete Boyer and before Nettles, third base for the Yankees was a veritable wasteland populated by a collection of mediocrities. They seemed to give any John, Rich, and Celerino a shot at winning the job; everyone from John Kennedy (they'd have been better off with Jackie), to Mike Ferraro, to Charlie Smith (obtained from the Cardinals in a swap for Roger Maris), to Bobby Cox (who was wise to move from the hot corner to the manager's office in Atlanta), to Rich McKinney (the Yankees' "big trade" in 1972 was to send Stan Bahnsen to the White Sox for McKinney; Bahnsen won 21 games for the Sox and McKinney batted .215, hit one home run, and drove in seven runs for the Yankees in 37 games and was gone a year later), and Celerino Sanchez (a one-year wonder).

The search for a third baseman, and the merry-go-round, ended with Nettles, who covered third base for the Yankees like snow in Fargo for eleven seasons and produced 250 home runs (10th on the Yankees all-time list) and 834 runs batted in (15th on the Yanks' all-time list). He set new standards in defense. His play in the 1978 World Series was considered on a par with Brooks Robinson's legendary performance at third base for the Baltimore Orioles in the 1970 World Series.

Nettles would play 22 major league seasons with six teams— the Yankees, Indians, Twins, Padres, Expos, and Braves—and his totals of 390 home runs and 1,314 RBI are Hall of Fame–worthy. In addition, he proved to be a student of the game, the possessor of a sharp eye, a player who was cunning and somewhat devious. Two incidents emphasize the point.

It was Nettles who noticed early in the 1983 season that his Kansas City Royals counterpart, third baseman George Brett, was using a bat in which the pine tar was slathered higher on the hitting surface than baseball rules allowed. Nettles brought his discovery to manager Billy Martin (they first got together in the minor leagues when Martin managed Nettles at Denver), who chose to file the information away and use it at the most propitious time. Such time came a few weeks later in Yankee Stadium when Brett smashed a seemingly game-winning home run against Goose Gossage. Martin reported Brett's offense to the umpires, who agreed that Brett used an illegal bat and called him out. And thus the so-called "Pine Tar Bat" incident was born.

Eventually, American League president Lee MacPhail overturned the umpire's ruling and Brett's game-winning home run was reinstated.

An earlier incident occurred on September 7, 1974, in Shea Stadium, the home of the New York Mets, which the Yankees used as their temporary residence during the 1974 and 1975 renovation of Yankee Stadium. The Yankees and Detroit Tigers played a doubleheader. In the second game, Nettles homered in his first at-bat. In his second at-bat, he blooped a hit to left field and as he did, the top of the bat flew off and several small rubber balls landed in foul territory between third base and home plate. The umpires called Nettles out for using an illegal bat. *That* umpires' ruling was upheld by the American League president.

I had long since been drawn to Nettles for several reasons. I wondered about his first name, an amalgamation of Craig and Gregg ("My mom was a lousy speller," he explained to my delight), was interested in the derivation of his nickname (his teammates called him "Puff" because he had a tendency to vanish from a crowd without an explanation as though he were a ghost or a magic dragon), and was intrigued by the self-deprecation he displayed by inscribing on his glove "E-5," the scorekeeper's shorthand in recording an error by the third baseman.

He had a tendency to display a sarcastic rapier tongue in an attempt to motivate his teammates, who, to a man, allowed him to apply his needle and not be offended. It's for that reason that Nettles served in the 1982 and '83 seasons as the Yankees' seventh captain between Thurman Munson and Willie Randolph.

Coincidentally (or not), the Yankees' improved fortunes seemed to dovetail with Nettles's presence. They went from a 79-win, fourth-place team the year before he arrived to a 100-win, World Championship team in five years. And they weren't done yet. In search of a third straight American League pennant and a second straight World Series title, they had signed Goose Gossage to a lucrative free agent contract in 1978 and turned their closer role over to him. But things didn't go well for Gossage once the season started. In the season opener in Texas, he came into a tie game in the ninth, and the first batter he faced, Richie Zisk, reached him for a game-winning home run. Unfortunately for Gossage, though, that wouldn't be the end of his pitching woes, and Nettles reportedly reminded him of it.

Three days after that season opener, Gossage entered in the sixth with a runner on first and the Yankees leading, 3–1, in Milwaukee. The first batter he faced, Larry Hisle, hit a home run to tie the score 3–3. In the seventh, the Brewers scored two more runs off Gossage for a 5–3 victory.

Seven days later in Toronto, Gossage entered in the fifth inning with the Yankees trailing the Blue Jays, 2–1. He gave up a sacrifice fly to make it 3–1, but the Yankees scored two in the sixth to tie the game at 3–3. However Gossage's misery continued in the ninth, when he was reached for a single and then made consecutive errors on two bunts to allow the winning run to score.

Four days later, Gossage was called in to pitch the eighth inning against the Brewers. When he arrived on the mound, he found Nettles waiting for him with a message of . . . support? . . . that only he could get away with.

"How are you going to screw this one up?" Nettles queried.

"I don't know," Gossage replied. "Why don't you go the (bleep) back to third base where you belong and we'll both find out?"

I had quickly found Nettles to be droll, clever, irreverent, sardonic, quick-witted, and eager to demonstrate those qualities, so it was little wonder that I began to make an obligatory daily stop at his locker in search of some gem. And more often than not he delivered, to wit:

When the Yankees traded Lyle to the Texas Rangers the year after he was voted winner of the American League Cy Young award, Nettles observed that "Sparky Lyle went from Cy Young to Sayonara."

When all hell kept breaking loose with the Yankees, he said, "Most kids grow up dreaming about playing Major League Baseball or joining the circus. I was lucky. I got to do both."

When the Yankees faced the Dodgers in the 1977 World Series and Nettles noted that Dodgers manager Tommy Lasorda had initiated the practice of hugging his players and the players hugging one another after a big hit, a great play in the field, or a victory, he commented, "The key to beating the Dodgers is to keep them from hugging each other."

When the Yankees told the players their attendance was mandatory at a particular promotional luncheon and Nettles adamantly refused and was fined, he remarked, "If they want somebody to play third base, they've got me. If they want somebody to go to luncheons, they can get George Jessel [at the time a famous entertainer and after dinner speaker known as "The Toastmaster General"]."

In an offhand remark, Nettles mused, "The best thing about playing for the Yankees is that you get to see Reggie Jackson play every day. The worst thing about playing for the Yankees is that you get to see Reggie Jackson play every day."

Nobody was too important, no star too big to avoid Nettles's barbs. Jackson was a particularly favorite foil for his needle, and, to Reggie's credit, he was intelligent enough to understand and appreciate Nettles's humor even when it was at his expense.

As a perfect example, there was an incident in an airport involving Nettles and Jackson. The Yankees were on a trip, going from one city to another, but their charter airplane had not yet arrived. To pass the time waiting for their charter plane, several players, including Nettles and Jackson, repaired to the airport watering hole. Along came a beautiful, well-dressed, obviously successful young African American businesswoman. Noticing the group of Yankees, she recognized Jackson and approached him politely.

"Mr. Jackson," the woman said, "I'm a big fan, and I just want to say hello and congratulate you on your career and wish you luck."

With that, the woman presented Jackson with her business card.

"If you're ever in my area," she said, "I'd appreciate if you called me and perhaps we can get together."

Noticing this exchange, and mindful of Jackson's preference in women, Nettles said, "It would help your chances if you have a blond wig."

Everybody laughed at Nettles's quip, Jackson harder than most.

# THIRTEEN

# TAKE MY WIFE, PLEASE!

The best time to be a baseball writer, no argument, is the six weeks or thereabouts of spring training. While New York and environs are buried in several feet of snow and his/her neighbors are schlepping to work in semi-darkness, sloshing through ice, slush, and sleet, bracing against hurricane-force winds and bundling up against subzero temperatures, the baseball writer is luxuriating in Florida's or Arizona's tropical climes, enjoying lazing on beaches, gentle breezes, dips in the ocean, and viewing the latest fashion in ladies' swimwear, or paucity thereof.

Serenity is the norm in the period from mid-February until April. Every team is undefeated, a World Series champion in waiting. Every player is a budding star. No batter is in a slump, no pitcher has lost a game, and hope springs eternal that "this will be the year."

Nothing much happens during spring training. Games are meaningless humdrum. Players go blithely through the motions and sit patiently for interviews with the media, delivering their answers to questions in platitudes. Mostly what happens in the six weeks of spring training is not newsworthy. Until it is!

We (those of us assigned by our newspapers to cover the Yankees' spring training) had arrived early as usual to the Yankees' spring training base at Fort Lauderdale Stadium on the morning of March 4, 1973, prepared for just another boring, balmy, lazy, uneventful, sun-splashed, eighty-degree day on Florida's Gulf Coast. Our objective: talk to a player or three, get a nice feature story, go back to the hotel, bat out the story, send it back to New York, and then hit the beach and continue critiquing the latest in ladies' swimwear.

As we circled inside the clubhouse and engaged in small talk with players, notebooks and pens at the ready, we were informed that there would be a press conference in twenty minutes in the office of manager Ralph Houk.

Ordinarily a press briefing four weeks before the start of the season meant some popular veteran had been told he was not going to make the team (too soon to make such a judgment), or had decided he couldn't cut it any longer and was announcing his retirement (what, give up that kind of money?), or some rookie had caught the eye of the manager and was told he would be going north with the team (unlikely; they hadn't even begun playing exhibition games yet).

The consensus was that the Yankees had called us together to announce a trade. We were right. The Yankees were announcing a trade, but, we soon discovered, it was not the conventional "my first baseman for your catcher" sort of trade. Not that sort of trade at all.

We entered the inner sanctum of Houk's office to find all the big brass waiting for us—Michael Burke, the Chief Executive Officer, he of the stylish long hair and expensive, tailored suits to match (George M. Steinbrenner III had headed up a group that purchased the team from the Columbia Broadcasting System only two months before, but he had not yet begun to display the demeanor that would lead to his sarcastic title of "the Boss" by sticking his nose where it didn't—or did—belong); Lee MacPhail, the general manager; Houk, the manager; and Robert O. Fishel, the team's genial and efficient director of public relations. The grim looks on their faces indicated this was not going to be a "Bully for us, look what we have accomplished" kind of press briefing.

The meeting was quickly commandeered by MacPhail, a droll, soft-spoken man who had spent the last thirty years as a baseball executive and who came from a baseball family (his father, Larry, had been the flamboyant, innovative, boisterous president/co-owner of the Brooklyn Dodgers, Cincinnati Reds, and New York Yankees). The son was no chip off the old block. He normally spoke in hushed tones, and now his tones were especially subdued as he related to us a tale so bizarre that it defied belief.

Two members of the Yankees pitching staff, Fritz Peterson, who had won 20 games in 1970 and 69 games over the past four seasons, and Mike Kekich, who had begun to fulfill the great promise predicted of him when he signed with the Los Angeles Dodgers as a nineteen-year-old nine years before by winning 10 games in each of the previous two years—both left-handers and such close friends that they were practically inseparable—had entered into an arrangement whereby they would trade wives. Not only would they trade wives, but they'd trade children, family pets, and residences as well; the children and pets had to remain with the mother and in their present house, the reason being, we were told, so as not to upset the childrens' lives.

Peterson would move in with Kekich's wife, Susanne, and her children in the Kekich home; Kekich would move in with

Peterson's wife, Marilyn, and her children in the Peterson home. Oh, and the dogs would go with the children, who so loved their pets. The intention, agreed to by all parties, was to obtain a divorce and marry each other's wives.

It would later be revealed that this all came to fruition during a lengthy late-night powwow among the four participants outside the home of sportswriter Maury Allen.

"Late in the 1972 season, I believe it was in August, I had a party at my house as I like to do every year," Allen remembered. "I usually invited some friends and other writers, and I liked to have a couple of ballplayers that I enjoyed being around. I invited Peterson and Kekich and their wives.

"Nothing unusual happened at the party, which broke up around midnight. My wife, Janet, and I were cleaning up. It was about two a.m., and we heard voices coming from the driveway outside the kitchen window. I looked out and there were the Petersons and Kekiches in a long conversation. I even mentioned to Janet that they were still there long after the party had broken up and all the other guests had left.

"I couldn't make out what they were talking about, so I just assumed they didn't want to leave that early and they were just enjoying some friendly chitchat. I never thought anything of it until it came out that they were trading families and I learned that what they were discussing outside my house that night was the arrangements and the details of their swap."

If the shocking announcement in Fort Lauderdale had come just twenty-seven days later we could easily have passed it off as April Fool's Day. As it was, there was some skepticism that this was a sham based on the fact that Peterson had gained a well-deserved reputation as a practical joker given his penchant for clubhouse pranks. (He would order merchandise out of a catalogue like fishing tackle or hunting rifles and have them sent to Thurman Munson at Yankee Stadium. When the items arrived and Munson opened the packages, he would blow his top that he was being charged for items he never purchased. All the while, Peterson was hiding around the corner watching Munson explode and trying not to laugh out loud.)

When Gene Michael was told about the "trade," his immediate reaction was to dismiss the rumor as just another prank.

"Those guys are pulling some trick again," he said. "Don't believe that stuff."

Believe it!

At the time, Marty Appel was a twenty-four-year-old assistant to Yankees PR Chief Fishel.

"I was not in Houk's office when the announcement was made," he recalled. "But I was involved when it was discussed what to tell the press."

Peterson had not yet arrived in the Yankees camp. He hadn't signed his contract and was officially declared a holdout. Kekich was in camp. Peterson heard that Kekich was telling the press about the switch, which was not true. Nevertheless, Peterson was on Florida's West Coast, and when he heard that Kekich was talking about the trade, he contacted Milton Richman of United Press International and unburdened himself to Milton, who put it on the wire. That set the wheels in motion and forced the Yankees' hand. They realized they had no choice but to fire a preemptive strike and call the team's beat writers together for a press briefing.

"The decision was made to level with the press," said Appel, "but to tell them this shouldn't be this big a story; it's a personal matter. It was also decided to exclude Sheila Moran (covering for the *New York Post* in her first spring training) because she was not a regular beat writer and was not one of 'the boys.' She would not understand and she would sensationalize it and put it all out of proportion. How can you put this story out of proportion?"

Both Peterson and Kekich suffered through bad seasons. It was clear that one of them had to go, and Kekich, being deemed the lesser pitcher of the two, drew the short straw. He had a record of 1–1 when on June 2, he was traded to the Cleveland Indians.

Meanwhile, Peterson and the Yankees had agreed on a new contract, but the distractions caused by the "trade" undoubtedly took their toll as he slipped from 17 wins in '72 to 8 in '73, the lowest win total in his eight-year major league career.

On April 26, 1974, Peterson was part of a blockbuster seven-player trade between the Yankees and Indians. Peterson was one of four pitchers the Yanks sent to Cleveland. However, twenty-nine days earlier, the Indians, undoubtedly in anticipation of obtaining Peterson in the trade and needing to avoid what would have been an awkward reunion, released Kekich, who quickly signed with the Texas Rangers. For their part in the seven-player deal with the Indians, the Yankees obtained Chris Chambliss, who had been voted American League Rookie of the Year in 1971 and who was in the fourth year of an efficient and admirably consistent major league career. He would become a fixture at first base for the Yankees over the next six years, a popular and solid citizen and a vital contributor to three Yankees pennants and two World Series championships.

Peterson enjoyed a slight resurgence in Cleveland, winning 23 games in two seasons, but on May 28, 1976, he became entwined once again with Kekich when he was traded to Texas (you can't make this stuff up). But, like the Indians, the Rangers avoided controversy and distractions by releasing Kekich two months before acquiring Peterson, who won one game for Texas and was released the following spring. He took one final shot at resurrecting his career by joining the Chicago White Sox during spring training, but failed to make the team and was cut, ending his playing career.

Kekich, however, managed one last hurrah with the Seattle Mariners, winning five games in 1977. But he was released the following spring and entered medical school in Mexico.

At last report, more than forty years after "the Trade," Peterson and Susanne were still together. Alas, Kekich and the former Marilyn Peterson didn't make it and parted shortly after "the Trade," another indication that only about 50 percent of baseball trades are deemed a success by both parties.

# FOURTEEN

# HAIL TO THE CHIEFS!

It came in the form of a letter on official White House stationery. The president of the United States wanted to see me.

Me?

Yes, me!

It was late September 1989, a few days before the start of the major league playoffs and the commander in chief, George H. W. Bush, was apparently suffering from baseball withdrawal, a common and understandable affliction for someone so consumed by other matters. For a bit of R&R and relief from the pressures of his job, the president thought it would be a good idea to invite twelve baseball writers and broadcasters (including Tim McCarver and Jerome Holtzman, then with the *Chicago Tribune*) to the White House for an informal chat about baseball.

I was privileged to be one of the twelve. If truth be told I understood that the reason I was included was that at the time I was president of the Baseball Writers Association of America and also because I represented the largest circulated daily newspaper in the country, the *New York Daily News*.

Our mission was to make our own arrangements to get to Washington, DC, and meet at the appointed hour at the visitors entrance to the White House. There we were checked in by members of the Secret Service. Once we had passed their scrutiny we were released to representatives of the President's press information staff who escorted us to a meeting room where we awaited the arrival of the most powerful man in the world.

After a few minutes, Mr. Bush swept into the room, where he greeted each of us warmly and cordially with a word of welcome and a handshake. As he did, a photographer snapped our picture. When the president had completed his tour of the room and greeted each of his guests, we sat around a large table and proceeded to have a discussion, led by the president, of one of his favorite subjects, baseball.

I found Mr. Bush to be more than just a casual fan. He was knowledgeable, conversant, and passionate about the game. In a forty-two-minute discussion he threw out names like Milt Pappas and George McQuinn. He knew that Don Zimmer once played for the Mets.

The popularity of sports in this country has prompted presidents who normally probably couldn't care less about such mundane matters to feign interest in the outcome of the World Series, the Super Bowl, or the NCAA basketball tournament. Because it affords a photo op in a joyous setting, such acts as throwing out the first ball to launch the baseball season is an obligatory chore for a United States president. How would it look for the country's leader to be absent each spring when our "national pastime" opens its season? There are votes at stake.

Consequently, since William Howard Taft began the tradition on April 14, 1910, for the game between the Washington Senators and Philadelphia Athletics, every sitting president has thrown out the first ball on opening day except Jimmy Carter (which is strange, because Carter would later throw out the first ball in Game 7 of the 1979 World Series and at the opening of San Diego's Petco Park in 2004, and in recent years he has been a regular attendee at Atlanta Braves games).

Most presidents have not been baseball buffs. They performed the first-ball-throwing chore out of a sense of duty and for the sake of public relations and appearances. Dwight D. Eisenhower preferred golf, John F. Kennedy played touch football and sailed, and Barack Obama is a basketball junkie.

Presidents Cleveland, Hoover, Clinton, and Roosevelt are not known for being rabid baseball fans, yet each has earned a niche in the game's lore.

It has been said that it was Grover Cleveland's young daughter Ruth, rather than the rising Yankees slugger George Herman (Babe) Ruth, for whom the Baby Ruth candy bar was named, a report that has proved to be decidedly apocryphal.

Similarly, it was Herbert Hoover that Babe Ruth was referencing when he was asked how it felt to be earning more money than the president of the United States and he famously replied, "I had a better year than he did."

In recent years, presidents have taken the first-ball ceremony more seriously. They're younger and more athletic than their predecessors, and they take the time to get their throwing arm in shape for their big baseball moment. On April 5, 1993, in the season opener between the Baltimore Orioles and the Texas Rangers in Camden Yards, President Clinton became the first president to successfully throw the first ball from the pitcher's mound to the catcher (it's a better photo op and a way to demonstrate one's athleticism to the voters). Prior to that, presidents either threw out the first ball from a box seat near the home team dugout or in front of the pitcher's mound.

Against the wishes of his closest advisers, President Bush the younger, who like his father is an avid baseball fan (he formerly was a part owner of the Texas Rangers), accepted an invitation from Major League Baseball to throw out the first ball prior to the start of Game 3 of the 2001 World Series between the Yankees and the Arizona Diamondbacks on October 30 in Yankee Stadium. Exactly seven weeks to the day earlier, some ten miles away in lower Manhattan, terrorist airplanes had deliberately crashed into the Twin Towers of the World Trade Center, leveling both buildings and killing thousands and thereby throwing the city, and the nation, into a state of panic and mourning.

Security was especially tight in and around the stadium that night, and the president would be vulnerable standing alone and unprotected on the pitcher's mound. If he insisted on going through with the pitch, his advisers urged him to at least wear a bulletproof vest. But Bush, a baseball purist, eschewed the vest on the grounds that it would negatively affect the throwing command of the commander in chief.

To ensure his ability to make a good, strong throw, the president arranged to take a few warm-up tosses under the stands in the bowels of the Stadium prior to the start of the game. As he was "warming up," Derek Jeter walked by.

"Hey, Mr. President," Jeter shouted. "Are you going to throw from the mound or from the front if it?"

"What do you think?" Bush replied.

"Throw from the mound or else they'll boo you," warned Jeter, who started walking away. Then suddenly he stopped, looked back, and said, "But don't bounce it. They'll boo you."

Mr. Bush heeded Jeter's advice. He didn't bounce his throw. He fired a perfect strike and headed triumphantly toward home plate, where he was greeted by the two managers, the Yankees' Joe Torre and Bob Brenly of the Diamondbacks as the huge Yankee Stadium crowd began spontaneously chanting, "USA . . . USA . . . USA."

Similarly, President Roosevelt earned the undying gratitude of sportsmen everywhere when, during the early days of World War II, he replied to those who called for the cessation of the baseball season during the conflict. In what became known as Roosevelt's "green light" letter to baseball commissioner Judge Kenesaw Mountain Landis on January 15, 1942, Roosevelt wrote:

*My dear Judge:*

*Thank you for yours on January fourteenth. As you will, of course, realize the final decision about the baseball season must rest with you and the Baseball club owners—so what I am going to say is solely a personal and not an official point of view.*

*I honestly feel that it would be best for the country to keep baseball going. There will be fewer people unemployed and everybody will work longer hours and harder than ever before.*

*And that means that they ought to have a chance for recreation and for taking their minds off their work even more than before.*

*Baseball provides a recreation which does not last over two hours or two hours and a half, and which can be got for very little cost. And, incidentally, I hope that night games can be extended because it gives an opportunity to the day shift to see a game occasionally.*

*As to the players themselves, I know you agree with me that the individual players who are active military or naval age should go, without question, into the services. Even if the actual quality to the teams is lowered by the greater use of older players, this will not dampen the popularity of the sport. Of course, if an individual has some particular aptitude in a trade or profession, he ought to serve the Government. That, however, is a matter which I know you can handle with complete justice.*

*Here is another way of looking at it—if 300 teams use 5,000 or 6,000 players, these players are a definite recreational asset to at least 20,000,000 of their fellow citizens—and that in my judgment is thoroughly worthwhile.*

*With every best wish,*

*Very sincerely yours,*

*Franklin D. Roosevelt*

(P.S. I personally am indebted to President Roosevelt, for it was in the 1942 season, on May 8, that I saw my first major league game in Ebbets Field, where my Dodgers beat those infernal New York Giants, 7–6.)

Taft, Richard Nixon, and Ronald Reagan, like both Bushes, were genuinely passionate about the game. Make whatever you will of this, but all five of those mentioned are/were Republicans. It is also interesting to note, and not surprising based on their party affiliations, that among the first-ball throwers, Taft, George W. Bush, Eisenhower, and Nixon were right-handed and Clinton and Obama are left-handed. What is surprising is that FDR, JFK, and Lyndon Johnson were right-handed and George Bush the elder is left-handed. Harry Truman, on the other hand, was ambidextrous and bipartisan. On opening day in 1950, Truman sat on the fence and threw out two first balls, one right-handed and one left-handed.

Taft, whose severest critics charged him with devoting more fervor following baseball than he did running the country, not only began the "first ball" ceremony, but also he is said to have started the seventh-inning stretch tradition on the same day. Midway through a pitching duel between the Senators' Walter Johnson and the Athletics' Eddie Plank, Taft (a huge man at six feet two inches tall and in excess of three hundred pounds) began to grow uncomfortable in the small wooden chair provided for him near the home team dugout. By the middle of the seventh inning, the president could abide the discomfort no longer, so he stood up to stretch his aching legs. Noticing the president rising, spectators also rose in a sign of respect for the leader of the country and the action on the field came to a halt. A few minutes later, Taft sat back down, the spectators did likewise, and the game continued.

Thus began a baseball tradition that continues to this day.

I became aware of Nixon's love of the game while covering the National League pennant race between the Dodgers and Giants in 1962. On October 1, Billy Pierce beat Sandy Koufax, 8–0, on a three-hitter and pitched the Giants into first place with one game to play. Nixon was there. He was running for governor of California against the incumbent Pat Brown. After the game, he came into the Giants' dressing room to congratulate and converse with Pierce. He drew a crowd of reporters who eavesdropped on the conversation between Pierce and Nixon. While there, Nixon claimed to be an old Chicago White Sox fan and proved it by naming the entire starting lineup of the 1936 Sox.

A decade later, then President Nixon released his all-time all-star baseball team, as selected with the aid of his son-in-law David Eisenhower, the grandson of President Ike. After he had retired and was living in nearby New Jersey, Nixon was a frequent guest in George Steinbrenner's private suite at Yankees games.

In the 1930s fans in and around Des Moines, Iowa, listened to broadcasts of Chicago Cubs games described in the warm, smooth voice of a young announcer called Ronald "Dutch" Reagan, who wasn't even at the ballpark. As was the custom of the day he would sit in a studio and recreate the play-by-play he received by Western Union teletype using sound effects to duplicate the crack of the bat and the roar of the crowd. From those humble beginnings as a sports announcer Reagan would move on to become one of the bright young stars of Hollywood in an era when actors such as Clark Gable, Gary Cooper, John Wayne, and Cary Grant were larger-than-life figures who invaded our consciousness and kept us entertained. But "Dutch" Reagan never forgot his roots or abandoned his love of sports. He starred as the ill-fated Notre Dame running back George Gipp in the film *Knute Rockne, All American* and as Grover Cleveland Alexander in the picture *The Winning Team*.

To this day when I read about the great Alexander, who was an epileptic and an alcoholic and won 373 major league games, the face I see is Ronald Reagan's. When Alexander strikes out Tony Lazzeri of the Yankees with the bases loaded and two outs in the seventh inning of the seventh game of the 1926 World Series in Yankee Stadium, it's not "Old Pete" Alexander throwing those pitches, but rather it's Ronald Reagan.

In 1966 Reagan was out of work (he would be elected governor of California that fall) and so was I, my newspaper having been ripped out from under me. I tried freelancing, books, magazine articles, and came up with the idea of contacting famous people from all walks of life and asking them to recount their best baseball memories. I sent one letter to Pacific Palisades, California.

About two weeks later, much to my surprise and utter delight, I received a letter in return. It has been hanging on my wall all these years. It's dated July 21, 1966, and it reads as follows:

"I don't think a single incident in any of the games I broadcast as a sports announcer impressed me so much as the last few weeks of the National League season, I believe it was '35 or '36 [ed. note: It was 1935]. At any rate, the Chicago Cubs came to a point where their only mathematical chance for winning the pennant lay in winding up the season, 21 games in all, without a defeat. I don't think anything in baseball has ever matched that.

"I was broadcasting the Cubs games at the time and as the totals started to mount, and they reached 15, and then 16, without a defeat, and you just couldn't believe it would happen, they went on and finished the season winning the last 21 games without a break." [Actually, the streak began on September 4 and ended on September 27. There were eight games remaining in the season, and the Cubs lost six of them, but they held on to win the pennant by four games over the St. Louis Cardinals and finished with a record of 100–54. However, in the World Series the Cubs were defeated by the Detroit Tigers, four games to two, and never won a World Series in "Dutch" Reagan's lifetime.]

While there have been United States presidents who played baseball for their college teams (most notably the older George Bush), none has ever played the game as a professional. It appeared in the 1980s and '90s that the United States might for the first time have such a person. Mario Cuomo, the fifty-second governor of New York, seemed to be on the fast track to the White House when he declined the Democratic Party's nomination in 1988 and 1992 and subsequently retired from politics.

Cuomo had been a varsity baseball player at St. John's University, an outfielder good enough to be scouted by the Pittsburgh Pirates and signed in 1952 for a bonus of $2,000. The Pirates sent him to Brunswick, Georgia, to play for their team in the class D Georgia-Florida League, where he batted .244 in 81 games.

Cuomo's baseball career was cut short when he was beaned by a pitch, convincing him to quit the game and enter law school.

Years later, Gov. Cuomo liked to tell friends that while he got $2,000 to sign with the Pirates, his signing bonus was $900 more than that which the Yankees at about the same time had offered a young outfielder from Oklahoma named Mickey Mantle.

Mantle once commented that the two dumbest scouts in baseball history were the one who signed Cuomo and the one who signed him.

"Cuomo was signed for two thousand dollars, and he never got out of class D," said Mantle. "I was signed for eleven hundred dollars and I made the Hall of Fame."

The older George Bush was born into privilege . . . and baseball. His uncle, George Herbert Walker (the former president is named after him) was part of the original ownership of the New York Mets, and as such, young George spent portions of a few spring trainings with the fledgling National League team.

Bush had been an outstanding player in his own right, a right-handed-batting, left-handed-throwing first baseman for the Yale Bulldogs. Bush's Yale team played in the first College World Series in 1947. For the inaugural World Series, the NCAA had divided the nation into two regional brackets, the eastern playoff with NYU, Clemson, Illinois, and Yale, and the western playoff with Texas, Oklahoma, Denver, and California.

Yale, with a record of 21–6, advanced to the finals in the east against the western division champion, California, which had a record of 29–10. In some places George Bush is listed as team captain for Yale (in others, it's Frank O'Brien Jr.), and apparently one of the perks of the job was meeting and posing for a picture with Babe Ruth in the Babe's declining days.

The World Series was a best-of-three series played not in Omaha, its future home, but on the campus of Western Michigan University in Kalamazoo. Cal won the first game, 17–4, and clinched the first NCAA baseball championship by winning the second game, 8–7, with future Yankee and Red Sox outfielder Jackie Jensen hitting the game-winning home run.

At his White House meeting with baseball writers and broadcasters in the fall of 1989 the president spoke little of his college baseball career, but his former coach Ethan Allen called him "a one-handed artist at first base," and a former Yale teammate, Dick Tettlebach, who played in the major leagues with the Yankees and Senators, said as a first baseman Bush was "absolutely superb; a real fancy Dan."

When I learned that I had been invited to join the group of journalists to indulge in a baseball conversation with the president, I arranged to have a gold metallic honorary BBWAA card made up inscribed with the president's name and present it to Mr. Bush. At the proper moment during our meeting, I requested the floor and made my presentation.

"Mr. President," I began, "as one president to another, I would like to present you with this honorary lifetime card of the Baseball Writers Association of America.

"With this card," I pressed on, "you can now gain admittance to any baseball stadium in this country."

My comment got the desired reaction from the president. He laughed!

Some weeks later there arrived at my home another letter on official White House stationery. It was dated December 22, 1989, and it read:

*Dear Phil:*

*I was delighted to welcome you and all the baseball sportscasters and journalists who attended the recent briefing at the White House. I enjoyed the informal discussion about this past season and America's favorite pastime in general.*

*I value that lifetime honorary gold card from the Baseball Writers' Association of America that you presented to me. Special thanks to you and your colleagues for this terrific remembrance.*

*With my best regards,*

*Sincerely,*

*George Bush*

This letter, like the one from "Dutch" Reagan, has been hanging on my wall all these years.

# FIFTEEN

# DESIGNATED HEBREW

It was born out of desperation, an experiment designed to boost sagging American League attendance at least temporarily. The designated hitter rule would be given a trial run after which the consensus assumed it would vanish from sight never to be seen—or even proposed—again.

That was more than forty years ago.

Baseball historians report that in 1906, after watching two of his star pitchers, Eddie Plank and Chief Bender, flail away futilely at bat, no less an authority than the legendary manager of the Philadelphia Athletics, Connie Mack, proposed a change in the rules that would permit a substitute batter (a designated hitter?) to take the place of the pitcher. Some say Mack was not the first to make such a proposal, but his stature gave the idea some traction. Still it never advanced past Mack's imagination.

In the 1920s, the president of the National League, John Heydler, tried to convince owners of the teams in his league to consider utilizing a "designated hitter" for the pitcher as a way to speed up the game, but like Mack's proposal, Heydler's never got off the drawing board.

There would be no more designated hitter talk for almost half a century until baseball took a dramatic downward turn in the late 1960s. In 1968, which would become known as "the year of the pitcher," major league baseball found itself in an alarming situation as pitchers dominated the game and attendance began to slip.

Denny McLain won 31 games for the Detroit Tigers, making him the first pitcher in thirty-four years to win at least 30 games. Seven other pitchers won at least 20 games. Seven pitchers recorded earned run averages under 2.00 with Bob Gibson of the St. Louis Cardinals compiling an all-time record ERA of 1.12 and Luis Tiant of the Cleveland Indians posting an all-time American League low of 1.60.

Carl Yastrzemski led the American League with the lowest average ever for a batting champion, .301 (no other American Leaguer batted higher than .290). And Willie McCovey's league-leading 36 home runs for the San Francisco Giants was the lowest total in 22 years for a National League home run king. Only three batters in both leagues drove in more than 100 runs.

Owners viewed the drop-off in attendance by 1.2 million patrons as a wake-up call. They concluded that fans preferred the 12–11 slugfest much more than they did the 2–1 pitchers duel and were attracted more by offense than by outstanding pitching, so they decided to do something to reverse the trend. For the 1969 season, the pitcher's mound would be lowered from fifteen feet to ten. While the change was agreed upon by both leagues, it was not enough to suit American League owners, who proposed including in the lineup an additional batter by employing a designated hitter for the pitcher, so instead of a pitcher that batted .165, they were hoping to replace him with a slugger capable of hitting 20–30 home runs.

Acting independent of one another, the American League, in a vote of 8–4, elected to approve the designated hitter for a trial period of three years beginning with the 1973 season. The National League opted to follow the party line and voted down the rule out of hand, choosing to continue with the status quo and thereby guaranteeing that, except for the World Series, All-Star games, and future interleague play, the two leagues would operate under different rules in DH perpetuity.

As spring training '73 began, American League managers, operating with no guidelines as precedent, were in search of candidates to fill the DH role. They would come from a cross-section of players that ranged from older veterans like Orlando Cepeda (Boston), Rico Carty (Texas), and Gates Brown (Detroit) to the physically compromised like Tony Oliva (Minnesota) and the defensively challenged.

The Yankees fell in the latter category, and to manager Ralph Houk the decision was a no-brainer. On his roster, Houk had a natural for the job.

In the throes of their worst five-year period in half a century, the Yankees in 1967 owned the first pick in the amateur draft and looked upon it as a rare opportunity to acquire the best amateur player in the land, one who would become a star and lead the Yankees to success for many years. They used the pick to select Ronald Mark Blomberg (pronounced "Bloomberg"), an eighteen-year old man-child from Atlanta, Georgia, with a chiseled muscular body, prodigious power, and a limitless upside. Not only was he a left-handed batter, which made him a perfect candidate to take aim at Yankee Stadium's easily reached right field seats, but he also came possessed with ideal ethnicity.

For years the Yankees had searched for a Jewish player, one who would be embraced by New York City's large Jewish population and who, coincidentally, would help the Yankees not only on the field but also at the box office. They had, to their everlasting shame and detriment, missed out on such Jewish stars and New York natives as Hall of Famers Hank Greenberg and Sandy Koufax, as well as other New Yorkers of the Jewish faith such as Sid Gordon, Cal Abrams, Saul Rogovin, and Harry Eisenstat. Now, in Ron Blomberg, they hoped they had a future Jewish star, one who had the talent to carry the Yankees to majestic, championship heights on his journey to Cooperstown.

*Kinehora!*

Blomberg quickly displayed his enormous promise with his bat, launching his professional career at Johnson City in the Appalachian Rookie League and moving steadily up the ladder as the Yankees put him on the fast track to the Bronx. When he opened eyes in 1971 with a .326 batting average for Syracuse of the AAA International League, the Yankees could hardly wait to bring him to the Bronx and put him in pinstripes. He arrived on June 24 and without missing a beat batted .322 for the Yankees with seven homers and 31 RBI in 64 games.

Before long, Blomberg was something of a folk hero. He was the embodiment of a budding Yankee superstar in the mold of Mickey Mantle, Joe DiMaggio, and Lou Gehrig, and he was polite, likeable, affable, engaging, and somewhat innocent. We in the media embraced him almost immediately. Most of us had never known a Jew with a drawl or someone with such a voracious appetite. One restaurant in Fort Lauderdale, the spring home of the Yankees, advertised there would be no charge for anyone who could devour its 72-ounce steak. Blomberg was more than equal to the challenge. He became a frequent patron of the restaurant until management identified the gluttonous customer and banned him.

Once when he grew frustrated because he was struggling at the plate Blomberg lamented that "I should never have become a baseball player. I should have become a doctor AND a lawyer like my mother and father wanted me to."

Meanwhile the Yankees tolerated his occasional slumps and tried desperately to find a position for him. They tried him in the outfield. Not a good idea. They tried him at first base. A worse idea! It required him to handle the baseball too often. Then, as if by some divine intervention, the American League rules makers provided the Yankees with the perfect solution. It was called the "designated hitter," and manager Ralph Houk announced in spring training 1973 that Blomberg would get the assignment. He was, in fact, born for the assignment; a born DH ("Designated Hebrew" according to the title of his autobiography).

Those of us covering the Yankees descended upon him for his thoughts. What did he think of his new role?

"I don't know," said our boy. "I've never done it before."

Duh! *Nobody* had ever done it before.

The Yankees were scheduled to open the season against the Red Sox in Boston on April 6, a 1 p.m. start. The starting lineups were as follows:

For the Yankees—Horace Clarke, 2b; Roy White, lf; Matty Alou, rf; Bobby Murcer, cf; Graig Nettles, 3b; Ron Blomberg, dh; Felipe Alou, 1b; Thurman Munson, c; Gene Michael, ss.

For the Red Sox—Tommy Harper, lf; Luis Aparicio, ss, Carl Yastrzemski, 1b; Reggie Smith, cf; Orlando Cepeda, dh; Rico Petrocelli, 3b; Carlton Fisk, c; Doug Griffin, 2b; Dwight Evans, rf.

The pitchers were Mel Stottlemyre for the Yankees and Luis Tiant for the Red Sox.

Because this game had the earliest scheduled starting time in the American League, the chances were good that Blomberg would officially be the first designated hitter in baseball.

When the first two Yankees were retired in the top of the first, it looked as though Blomberg might not come to bat in the inning and Cepeda could beat him to history. But Matty Alou doubled and Tiant, in a rare display of wildness, walked Murcer and Nettles. That brought Blomberg to bat.

History arrived quietly, in the form of a run-scoring base on balls.

After the game, Marty Appel, the Yankees' assistant director of public relations, had the foresight to ask Blomberg for his bat, which was sent to the Baseball Hall of Fame and Museum in Cooperstown, New York.

"I've been there a few times," said Blomberg, "and the bat is on display with my name as the first designated hitter in baseball history. It's a funny way to make the Hall of Fame."

Said Marty Appel: "It's the only bat in the Hall of Fame that commemorates a base on balls."

# SIXTEEN

# OLD MAN RIVERS

See Mick walk!

See him slowly shuffle along on tippy-toes, bent over from the waist, head down, taking mincing little steps and looking like he's wearing a pair of shoes two sizes too small.

See Mick bat!

He swings and misses and twirls the bat with all the dexterity of a prize-winning college drum majorette at the big Saturday football game.

See Mick run!

See him hit the baseball and take off, no longer bent over from the waist, no longer looking like he's wearing a pair of shoes two sizes too small, a man on a mission, trying to get somewhere fast, flying around the bases at breakneck speed.

It is why they call John Milton (Mickey) Rivers "Mick the Quick," why he was able to lead the American League in triples in two consecutive seasons and in stolen bases once, why in 1976, the Yankees traded Bobby Bonds, a potential Hall of Famer, to the California Angels in exchange for Mick and pitcher Ed Figueroa.

Mickey Rivers would become the latest in a more than fifty-year nearly unbroken string of outstanding Yankees center fielders, from Earle Combs to Joe DiMaggio to Mickey Mantle to Mickey Rivers. All three of his Yankees center field predecessors made the Hall of Fame. Rivers merely won championships. He was an instrumental part of the Yankees ending a twelve-year drought and winning three consecutive American League pennants and two World Series.

The trade that brought Rivers to the Yankees also brightened my life and made my job a little easier. I found Mick the Quick to be an engaging and warm-hearted fellow, a gentle soul and an irrepressible wit, all of it belying the impression I formed of him before I got to know him. I have long maintained that the only person Mickey Rivers ever harmed is Mickey Rivers.

Mick the Quick came to the Bronx, New York, and hit the ground running—his mouth, that is—thereby forever endearing himself to his teammates and members of the traveling press with his razor-sharp observation of no less an icon than Reggie Jackson.

"Reginald Martinez Jackson," The Quick commented one memorable day on one memorable bus ride heading to the airport on one memorable trip. "You got a white man's first name, a Spanish man's second name, and a black man's third name. You all (bleeped) up."

It wasn't long before Rivers was being recognized, and hailed, as the team's resident raconteur, wit, and philosopher.

"Ain't no sense worrying about things you got control over 'cause if you got control over them, ain't no sense worrying," he reasoned. "And there ain't no sense worrying about things you got no control over, 'cause if you got no control over them, ain't no sense worrying about them."

Now I offer in evidence that there ain't no sense questioning that kind of logic!

Like Babe Ruth and Casey Stengel, Rivers had difficulty remembering names. While Ruth called everyone "Kid" and Stengel called everyone "Doctor," Rivers addressed teammates, writers, and anyone associated with the Yankees with the affectionate (?) greeting "Gozzlehead" (Rivers addressed me by that name often, but not once did I feel complimented), and as is the wont of baseball people, they in turn called Rivers "Gozzlehead." Rivers said he first heard the term as a child in the Miami ghetto and claims it means a funny-looking creature, "You know, like a bullfrog face."

When we writers were permitted to ride the team bus to and from the ballpark, the airport, and the hotel, we found Rivers's exchanges with Jackson a hilarious source of entertainment. They were the Yankees' Odd Couple, Rivers a poor ghetto kid from Miami, Jackson a college-educated son of a Philadelphia tailor from a middle-class Philadelphia suburb who boasted that he possessed an IQ of 160.

"Out of what, a thousand?" Rivers queried.

"Look at this," Reggie replied. "I'm arguing with a guy that can't even read or write."

"Well, you better stop readin' and writin' and start hittin'," Rivers suggested.

One day in the visitor's clubhouse in Milwaukee County Stadium I overheard a conversation between Rivers and Carlos May, a left-handed-hitting outfielder who had been traded to the Yankees by the White Sox early in the '76 season. Inevitably, their discussion got around to which of the two had the higher IQ, until May brought the discussion to a roaring halt when he hit Rivers with, "You don't even know how to spell IQ."

On the field, Rivers was everything he was reported to be in his first year as a Yankee. He batted .312, had 187 hits, scored 95 runs, hit eight triples, stole 67 bases, and roamed center field with aplomb and blanket coverage. The Yankees might not have finished first in the American League East without Mick the Quick. He was third in the American League Most Valuable Player Award voting (behind his teammate Thurman Munson and George Brett of the Kansas City Royals), but in an informal vote of his teammates, Rivers and Munson were tied for the top spot.

In the spring of 1977, Rivers reflected on his first season in pinstripes and looked ahead to his second season.

"We'll do all right if we can capitalize on our mistakes," he said. "My goals are to hit three hundred, score a hundred runs, and stay injury-prone."

The Quick made good on two of his three goals. He did bat .300 (.326 to be exact, good for fourth in the American League behind Rod Carew and Lyman Bostock of the Minnesota Twins and Ken Singleton of the Baltimore Orioles), but he scored only 79 runs largely because he was "injury prone," having missed 24 games. But the Yankees won 100 games, finished 2½ games ahead of Baltimore in the AL East, and won their first World Series in fifteen years.

Along the way, Rivers conducted a few lectures on the atmosphere—"The first thing you do when you get out to center field is put up your finger and check the wind-chill factor"—and there was the day early in the 1978 season when Rivers managed to get under the skin of relief ace Rich (Goose) Gossage, while at the same time tickling the fancy of his teammates, the press, and the fans.

Gossage had signed with the Yankees that year as a free agent, but his start in pinstripes was less than auspicious. He had blown leads in his first three appearances. On May 3, Gossage was summoned by Billy Martin in the top of the ninth inning against the Kansas City Royals at Yankee Stadium to protect a 6–5 lead.

The routine in those days was for a car decorated in pinstripes to drive to the bullpen, pick up the relief pitcher, and deliver him to the pitcher's mound. In center field, Mickey Rivers's mind was working overtime. He watched the car drive to the bullpen, slightly to the right of center field. He watched the bullpen gate swing open. He watched as Gossage came striding purposefully toward the car.

At that moment, Rivers sprinted toward the bullpen auto and draped his skinny frame on the car's hood, as if to say, "No, no, don't bring him in. Not HIM!"

Everybody had a good laugh, except Gossage. But Mick's prank had its desired effect, as Gossage retired the Royals in order in the ninth, with two strikeouts and a fly ball to left, to collect his first save as a Yankee.

In his three and a half seasons as a Yankee, Mickey Rivers left quite an impressive legacy. In addition to three American League pennants and two World Series championships in his three full seasons, he had a three-year batting average of .301, had 516 hits, scored 252 runs, hit 21 triples, stole 184 bases, and left a boatload of friends and wonderful memories like the time his wife, Mary, tried to run him down with her car in the players' parking lot. She failed because luckily the Mick was too Quick.

Rivers was especially productive in clutch situations. He seemed to save his best games for the Yankees' biggest games. In 14 games in the American League Championship Series, he belted out 22 hits, scored 10 runs, and batted .386. Of particular note and a major part of the Rivers legacy was the 1977 ALCS against the Kansas City Royals.

Down two games to one in the best-of-five series, the Yankees were faced with having to win two games in Kansas City. In Game 4, Rivers had 4 hits and scored twice, and the Yankees won, 6–4. So it all came down for the American League pennant to a winner-take-all final game.

Going into the ninth inning of Game 5, the Yankees trailed, 3–2. Paul Blair opened the inning with a single and Roy White walked, bringing up Rivers, who slashed a single to right field to score Blair with the tying run. White would score on Willie Randolph's sacrifice fly, and Rivers would score on an error by third baseman George Brett, giving the Yankees a 6–4 victory and sending them to the World Series for the third straight year.

What was later revealed was that Rivers had threatened to sit out the climactic fifth game unless he got a cash advance on his future salary. It was a frequently used and usually successful ploy by Rivers, who had a particular fondness for four-legged animals, especially those making frequent appearances at local ovals which housed pari-mutuel windows.

Rivers knew when to use his secret weapon and on whom he should use it—the owner of the Yankees, George M. Steinbrenner, who had affection for Rivers ("He's a sweet, sweet kid"), shared in Rivers's fondness for four-legged animals and was willing to do whatever it took to win.

Often Rivers would repair to the trainer's room and threaten to stay there through the full nine innings if the team did not accede to his wishes for an advance of his salary. (The joke around the Yankees was that Rivers was already being paid for several years after he had retired.) A few minutes later a messenger would arrive from Steinbrenner's office or his luxury suite with a white envelope stuffed with pieces of paper upon which were pictures of dead presidents (No Lincolns or Washingtons among them).

Eventually, Steinbrenner tired of the "sweet, sweet kid" and his constant demands, and Rivers was traded to the Texas Rangers on July 30, 1979. Mick left the Yankees reluctantly and sadly. He loved the big city, the Yankees, his teammates, his friends, his fans, and the local ovals (Texas had no such playgrounds). And the Yankees, his teammates, his friends, his fans, and several proprietors of the local ovals, who would soon discover a mysterious decline in their daily mutual handle, loved him.

I caught up with Rivers the following spring in Pompano Beach, Florida. He tried to put on a brave façade, but it was apparent he was somewhat downcast over the sudden change in his life. I tried to assuage his disappointment by pointing out that the Yankees are notorious for bringing back their old heroes.

I reminded him that Steinbrenner had brought Martin back the previous year after firing him the year before.

"You know that George and Billy always liked you," I said.

My comment brought a smile to Rivers's face.

"Yeah," he agreed. "Me, George, and Billy, we two of a kind."

# SEVENTEEN

# SAY WHAT?

The New York Yankees are not only the richest, most successful, most prestigious, most admired, and most popular professional sports team in the United States, but also they are the most talked-about and their players, managers, coaches, and executives are the most quoted.

Following are some of the most frequently and well-known utterances emanating from Yankeeland.

*"WHEN THE YANKEES SCORE EIGHT RUNS IN THE FIRST INNING AND SLOWLY PULL AWAY."*
—COL. JACOB RUPPERT, when asked what he considered to be the perfect day at the ballpark.

Ruppert, a native New Yorker, was a beer baron and a four-term United States congressman who partnered with another colonel, Tillinghast L'Hommedieu Huston, to purchase the Yankees from Frank Farrell and Bill Devery for the princely sum of $480,000 in 1915. At the time, the Yankees were an American

League bottom feeder, but under Ruppert (who would buy out Huston eight years later for $1.5 million) the Yankees would become an American League power.

Not one to stint on spending to improve his product, Ruppert would use his wealth to purchase Babe Ruth from the Red Sox (later he also approved the purchase of a Columbia University first baseman named Lou Gehrig and a young center fielder from the San Francisco Seals of the Pacific Coast League, Joe DiMaggio). He also endorsed the selection of Miller Huggins and Joe McCarthy as managers.

Ruppert is credited with purchasing ten acres of swampland in the Bronx for $1.5 million upon which he built a state-of-the-art, three-tier, seventy-thousand-seat ballpark and named it Yankee Stadium. And it was Ruppert who designed the Yankees' pinstriped home uniforms and who enabled the Yankees to become the first team to put numbers on the backs of those uniforms.

Ruppert maintained ownership of the Yankees until his death on January 13, 1939, five and a half months before a dying Lou Gehrig made his farewell address at Yankee Stadium.

Before Ruppert came aboard, the Yankees/Highlanders had finished higher than fifth place just three times and had never won a championship. Under Ruppert's ownership, they won ten pennants and seven World Series. Ruppert was elected to the Baseball Hall of Fame in 2013, seventy-three years after his death.


*"WE PLAN ABSENTEE OWNERSHIP. WE'RE NOT GOING TO PRETEND WE'RE SOMETHING WE AREN'T. I'LL STICK TO BUILDING SHIPS AND LET THE BASEBALL PEOPLE RUN THE TEAM."*
—GEORGE M. STEINBRENNER III, on January 3, 1973, the day it was announced that the Cleveland shipbuilder headed up a

group that purchased the New York Yankees from the Columbia Broadcasting System for $10 million.

So much for best laid plans and broken promises!

*"TODAY, I CONSIDER MYSELF THE LUCKIEST MAN ON THE FACE OF THE EARTH."*

—LOU GEHRIG, dying of amyotrophic lateral sclerosis, later to be termed "Lou Gehrig's Disease," on July 4, 1939, "Lou Gehrig Day" at Yankee Stadium. Gehrig would die less than two years later, on June 6, 1941, thirteen days short of his thirty-eighth birthday.

*"I HAD A BETTER YEAR THAN HOOVER."*

—BABE RUTH, when asked in 1930 by a sportswriter how it felt to be earning more money ($80,000) than the $75,000 paid Herbert Hoover, the president of the United States.

*"POOR BABE, HE'S HAVING A BAD YEAR."*

—WHITEY FORD, on October 8, 1961, after pitching five shutout innings against the Cincinnati Reds in Game 4 of the World Series to run his Series consecutive scoreless record to 33 ⅔ innings, breaking the World Series record of 29⅔ innings set by Babe Ruth of the Boston Red Sox forty-three years earlier. Just weeks before Ford broke Ruth's World Series pitching record, the Babe's single season home run record of 60 was broken by Ford's teammate, Roger Maris.

*"I'LL NEVER MAKE THE MISTAKE OF BEING SEVENTY AGAIN."*

—CASEY STENGEL, upon being fired by the Yankees on October 18, 1960, eighty days after his seventieth birthday, presumably because he was deemed too old to continue in the job, although he had led the Yankees to their tenth pennant in his twelve-year reign and lost the World Series to the Pittsburgh Pirates in seven games. Said Stengel: "I commenced winning pennants when I came here, but I didn't commence getting any younger." Two years later Stengel was named manager of the expansion New York Mets of the National League.

*"IT'S GREAT TO BE YOUNG AND A YANKEE."*
—WAITE HOYT was nicknamed "Schoolboy" because he was precocious—he reached the big leagues and appeared in a game at age eighteen. Hoyt was born in Brooklyn and signed as a free agent with the New York Giants. He spent two seasons with the Boston Red Sox and was traded to the Yankees after the 1920 season, one year after Babe Ruth arrived also from Boston.

At age twenty-one in 1921, Hoyt won 19 games and helped the Yankees win their first American League pennant. In the 1921 World Series against the New York Giants, Hoyt won Game 2, 3–0, on a two-hitter, won Game 5, 3–1, but in the deciding Game 8, he was the hard luck losing pitcher, 1–0, on an unearned run in the first inning.

Hoyt would win 157 games in ten seasons with the Yankees and compile 237 wins for seven teams in a twenty-one-year career. He was elected to the Hall of Fame in 1969.

*"I WANT TO THANK THE GOOD LORD FOR MAKING ME A YANKEE."*
—JOE DIMAGGIO
The famous quote by the legendary "Yankee Clipper" is on a sign that for many years hung in the runway leading from the Yankees clubhouse to the dugout in the old Yankee Stadium

and was moved into the new stadium. It purports to have been spoken by DiMaggio in October 1941, the year he hit in his record 56-consecutive games. However, there is evidence to dispute the date.

On October 1, 1949, the Yankees staged "Joe DiMaggio Day" at the stadium and the honoree, suffering from a virus, crawled out of a hospital bed to appear at the celebration and include the famous quote in his speech to the fans.

*"I THOUGHT I RAISED A MAN. I SEE I RAISED A COWARD INSTEAD. IF THAT'S ALL THE GUTS YOU HAVE YOU CAN COME BACK TO OKLAHOMA AND WORK IN THE MINES WITH ME."*
—MUTT MANTLE, Mickey's father

Highly touted as the heir apparent to Joe DiMaggio as the Yankees center fielder and resident superstar, things were not going well for Mickey Mantle in 1951, his rookie season. In 69 games the nineteen-year-old wunderkind was batting a non-superstar-like .260 with seven home runs, 45 RBI, and an alarming 52 strikeouts.

On July 13, he was sent to the Yankees' Kansas City farm team in search of his batting stroke. Upon arriving in KC, Mantle called home and poured his heart out to his father, expressing his discouragement and questioning his career choice. Mutt Mantle listened to his son's lament and then told him not to do anything rash: "I'm on my way."

Mutt Mantle got in the family car and drove nonstop from Commerce, Oklahoma, to Kansas City. Upon his arrival, Mutt began packing Mickey's clothes in a suitcase. When Mickey asked his father what he was doing, Mutt uttered the now famous quote that was both a challenge and an ultimatum, which had the desired effect.

When Mutt mentioned taking his son back to Oklahoma with him, where the young Mantle could join his father working in the mines, Mickey had a change of heart and chose to stay in Kansas City, where his bat came alive in Kansas City. In 40 games, he batted .361 with 11 homers and 50 RBI, earning him a recall by the Yankees to stay and to become the superstar that had been predicted of him.

### *"THE ONLY PLACE DEREK JETER IS GOING IS COOPERSTOWN."*
—DICK GROCH, a Yankees scout

As they prepared for the 1992 major league free agent draft, the Yankees were swimming in a sea of mediocrity. They would fail to finish in first place for the twelfth straight year, and they would finish no higher than fourth place for the sixth straight year.

Having finished in fifth place in the American League East the previous year with 71 wins, the Yankees were in line to select sixth in the draft and hopeful that would produce a top-flight prospect they might have for many years. A No. 6 pick was considered much too precious to waste.

At a meeting of Yankees personnel concerned with player development, Dick Groch, a veteran Yankees scout assigned to cover the Ohio-Michigan territory was lavish in his praise of a tall, skinny, not quite eighteen-year-old shortstop for Kalamazoo (Mich.) Central High School named Derek Jeter. Groch pushed hard for the Yankees to consider taking Jeter should he still be available when their turn came up. (Partly because he has conviction in his judgment and partly as a tactic to justify his position, it's not uncommon for a scout to argue fervently in support of his free agent prospect.)

"Jeter?" piped up someone at the meeting. "Isn't he going to the University of Michigan?"

To which Groch made his now famous, clairvoyant comment.

*"THERE IS ALWAYS SOME KID WHO MAY BE SEEING ME FOR THE FIRST TIME OR THE LAST TIME. I OWE HIM MY BEST."*

—JOE DIMAGGIO, when asked by a sportswriter why he continued to hustle and play hard at the risk of injury late in his career after he had accomplished so much and established himself as one of the game's all-time greats.

*"ONE'S A BORN LIAR AND THE OTHER'S CONVICTED."*

—BILLY MARTIN, speaking of Reggie Jackson (the "liar") and George Steinbrenner. Steinbrenner was convicted in 1974 for making illegal contributions to Richard Nixon's reelection campaign.

It was July 23, 1978. The Yankees had completed a three-game sweep in Chicago by beating the White Sox in an afternoon game after which they left for O'Hare Airport to board their charter for their trip to Kansas City. The Yankees had completed their three-game sweep without Jackson. He had returned that day after sitting out a five-game suspension imposed by Martin when Reggie, in an act Martin deemed as gross insubordination, had ignored the manager's bunt sign.

The Yankees had won all five games Jackson missed and Martin, emboldened by success and his tongue loosened by alcohol, made his ill-advised "born liar" and "convicted" remark.

The next day, in Kansas City, Martin announced his resignation as manager of the Yankees.

*"I'D WALK INTO THE OWNER'S OFFICE, SHAKE HIS HAND, AND SAY, 'HIYA, PARTNER.'"*
—JOE DIMAGGIO, when asked how much he would be worth if he were playing today.

*"I WASN'T HIRED TO PUT ON A FAREWELL TOUR."*
—JOE GIRARDI, MANAGER OF THE YANKEES, when asked after not starting Derek Jeter against the Boston Red Sox on April 12, 2014, if it concerned him that he might be alienating some fans who bought tickets to the game hoping to see Jeter, who had announced he would retire after the 2014 season, play for the last time.

*"IF I HAD KNOWN IT WAS A BIG DEAL, I'D HAVE DONE IT EVERY YEAR."*
—MICKEY MANTLE, after hearing in 1988 that Jose Canseco was the first player in baseball history to hit 40 home runs and steal 40 bases in the same season. Mantle hit 40 or more home runs four times in his career, but while he was blessed with blazing speed, he also suffered from leg and knee problems that prevented him from stealing more than 21 bases in any one season.

*"BOOOO!"*
—MOST IN THE YANKEE STADIUM CROWD OF 37,484 each time former Yankee Robinson Cano came to bat on April 29, 2014. Clearly they were booing Cano because they considered him greedy, a turncoat, and an ingrate (they even chanted, "You sold

out") because Cano committed the unpardonable sin of turning down the Yankees' offer of $175 million to sign with the Seattle Mariners for $65 million more. These are many of the same fans who have cheered Brian McCann, Carlos Beltran, Jacoby Elsbury, and before them CC Sabathia and Mark Teixiera, who walked away from other teams to sign with the Yankees for more money.

# EIGHTEEN

# THE MICK

When Mickey Mantle passed away on August 13, 1995, one eulogist marked his passing as "the end of our innocence." Another, sportscaster Bob Costas, said he was "the most compelling baseball hero of our lifetime." Still another called him "the last American hero."

Mickey Charles Mantle, born in Oklahoma, hero of the Bronx, New York, was all of that and more. He was bigger than life, although he stood only five feet, eleven inches tall. He seemed to possess superhuman strength, although he weighed only 195 pounds. He was a towering figure who captured the fans' fancy by hitting monstrous, majestic, towering, prodigious home runs. The two most notable, of course, came on April 17, 1953, a tremendous blast in Washington's Griffith Stadium batting right-handed against Chuck Stobbs of the Senators that reportedly traveled 565 feet and a missile on May 22, 1963, hit left-handed against Kansas City's Bill Fischer that came within inches of clearing the 108-foot-1-inch-high third deck in right field and being the only ball hit out of venerable Yankee Stadium. The Mick was also a study in contrasts, irascible and affable, rude and generous, boorish and engaging, meanspirited and compassionate, profane and witty.

He was ordained for greatness at birth. He was "Mickey," not Michael or Mike, named for Gordon Stanley (Mickey) Cochrane, the great Hall of Fame catcher for the Detroit Tigers and the favorite player of Mantle's father, Mutt, who also had the good sense and foresight to make his son into a switch-hitter. ("I'm glad my dad didn't name me Gordon," Mantle often said.)

The name Mutt Mantle gave his boy was catchy, alliterative (MM), and synchronized, six letters in each of his first two names. As someone pointed out, if you drop the first three letters of his first name and the last three letters of his last name, what do you have? KEY MAN, which he was for the Yankees almost from the day he arrived in New York, a nineteen-year-old blonde baseball Adonis.

On July 8, 1958, we got our first glimpse of what would become a Mantle trademark, his quirky, irreverent sense of humor that he would often accompany with a crinkling of his nose. With the annual All-Star Game being played the previous day in nearby in Baltimore, American League manager Casey Stengel and Mantle were summoned to Washington, DC, to appear before the Senate Anti-trust and Monopoly Subcommittee chaired by twice-defeated presidential candidate Sen. Estes Kefauver.

After Stengel's interminable, long-winded, discombobulated, circuitous, and unfathomable discourse in which he tiptoed, dodged, and cleverly begged the question by tracing his life and career in his unique language described as "Stengelese," Sen. Kefauver, confounded and confused, gave up. He decided he had a better chance of getting what he wanted from Mantle and turned to the Yankees' young center fielder.

"Mr. Mantle, do you have any observations with reference to the applicability of the antitrust laws to baseball?"

"My views," said Mantle, "are just about the same as Casey's."

I knew Mantle for more than three decades, first casually as a reporter charged with covering the Yankees and Mantle, their biggest star, and later more intimately as the ghost writer for his book that chronicled his Triple Crown season, 1956. In those thirty-plus years I would witness the gamut of the Mantle personality, and I would see him morph from a shy, naïve, uneducated, simple country boy into an urbane, sophisticated, worldly man-about-Manhattan.

I accompanied him on book-signing appearances. At one venue I watched in amazement as a man in his fifties welled up with tears and was struck speechless at merely coming face-to-face with his boyhood idol. I cringed when Mantle grew impatient, restless, and hostile and insulted one fan who lingered too long in front of him. I experienced many examples of rudeness by Mantle in my early encounters with the Yankees star.

His crass behavior brought back memories of being a young reporter joining in the crowd in front of Mantle's locker to interview him after he had led some Yankee victory, performed some magical feat on the diamond, and hit still another of his majestic home runs. He would sit on the stool at his locker and answer question after question affably and humorously until he felt he had given enough of himself. Then he would pull himself up from the stool and without a word of explanation or apology, walk away leaving the crowd of reporters baffled and unsatisfied.

Looking back, I came to realize that I went through three stages of conclusions in assessing Mantle's odd behavior.

At first I thought him rude, crude, and uncouth.

Later, after watching him wrap his battered legs before each game and limp around the clubhouse or grab hold of a railing as he climbed on and off the team bus, I attributed his rudeness to the fact that he was in constant pain. At the same time I became aware that he was abusing alcohol as a means of self-medication against the pain and realized that the booze was often controlling his personality in a negative way.

Still later, after he had retired and his pain had abated somewhat and the pressure to perform on the field no longer was driving him, he was much more likable, a joy to be with. I got to know him better and I came to believe that what I attributed to rudeness, physical pain, and alcohol that caused him often be insufferable when he was a player was really his insecurity and humility. I concluded that he never thought he was worthy of such hero worship—that he was not a god, he was a baseball player, nothing more.

That humility surfaced in 1995 in New York City's Sheraton Hotel and Towers on a cold winter night in January. The New York Chapter of the Baseball Writers Association of America had instituted an annual award to be called "The Willie, Mickey & the Duke," designed to recognize and honor players who were bound together by some common thread. Fittingly, the first winners of the "Willie, Mickey & the Duke" award were Willie, Mickey, and the Duke, center fielders, and icons, with the three New York baseball teams in the 1950s (Willie Mays with the New York Giants, Mickey Mantle with the New York Yankees, and Duke Snider with the Brooklyn Dodgers), and each a member of Baseball's Hall of Fame. They would come together for what would be the last time—Mantle would die less than seven months later—to accept their award.

In his acceptance speech, Mantle commented that when people talked about the three New York center fielders and fans debated endlessly about which of the three was the greatest, they were spinning their wheels. Mickey had it all figured out and he was prepared to tell the world that of the three, the greatest, no argument, no dispute, was Willie.

Having made this pronouncement in front of a crowd of more than 1,100 and seeking affirmation, Mantle turned to Snider and asked, "Isn't that right, Duke?" And Snider could be seen vigorously nodding his head in agreement.

When Mantle and I began working on his book, and I got to spend a lot more time with him, I gained a new appreciation of him, a side I had never before seen. He was warm, considerate, compassionate, and the possessor of a wonderful, childlike sense of humor. I looked forward to our times together.

We would meet on his visits to New York, and we would discuss material to be included in his book, which I would work on when he was gone. When he returned to New York, we would go over the chapters for him to approve or disapprove.

These meetings would take place at the restaurant that bore his name or in the posh midtown hotel where he was staying. They usually involved a meal and, although he knew I had an expense account, Mantle would never allow me to pick up a check. The Mickey Mantle I choose to remember most fondly was the one with whom I one day shared a working brunch.

There were four of us—Mantle, his manager/companion, me, and my lady friend.

On this day, Mantle was at his most charming and most amusing. It was easily apparent he was in a good mood. We worked and we laughed, usually at his slightly ribald humor.

As we were about to leave, we became aware of a commotion at a nearby table involving hotel personnel and a patron, an elderly, neatly and expensively dressed gentleman.

Curious, Mantle asked the waiter what the hubbub was all about. He was told that the elderly gentleman had feasted on a sumptuous brunch complete with two bottles of expensive wine, but when he was presented with the check, in the range of $95, he confessed that he had no money.

At that point Mantle gestured slightly with his hand. He had asked for the old gent's check, which he then paid.

# NINETEEN

# FOUR S(CORE)

When the Yankees traded Elston Howard to the Boston Red Sox on August 3, 1967, for the immortal Ron Klimkowski and Pete Magrini, it marked the sad end of a memorable era. The trade effectively broke up a triumvirate of Yankees legends. Howard, Mickey Mantle, and Whitey Ford had spent their entire major league careers with the Yankees and had played together as teammates for 13 seasons, 1955–67, the first such trio of Yankees to play 13 uninterrupted seasons as teammates since Bill Dickey, Lefty Gomez, and Red Ruffing (each a member of the Hall of Fame) in 1930–42.

A quarter of a century after the Howard-Mantle-Ford breakup, we stood in awe as three members of the Milwaukee Brewers, Hall of Famers Robin Yount and Paul Molitor, and Jim Gantner, completed a string of fifteen consecutive seasons as teammates and believed we were seeing the last of a breed.

As Major League Baseball moved into the era of expansion, interleague play, interleague trading, and free agency, it seemed unlikely we would ever again witness that particular phenomenon of unity and camaraderie.

But we were wrong. Boy, were we wrong. Emphatically so!

As the three Milwaukee Caballeros were completing their unlikely streak, the Yankees, who were stumbling through their fourth consecutive losing season, were completing the process of replenishing a nearly depleted minor league system by using the sixth pick in the 1992 first-year-player draft to select a skinny high school shortstop named Derek Sanderson Jeter from Kalamazoo, Michigan.

Jeter was considered a top-flight prospect, so much so that no less an authority and skilled talent evaluator than the Houston Astros' Michigan-area scout Hal Newhouser was willing to put his reputation on the line for the young shortstop.

Newhouser had starred as a wartime pitcher with the Detroit Tigers, winning 29, 25, and 26 games in 1944–45–46 and being voted the American League Most Valuable Player in 1944 and '45. So taken with Jeter was Newhouser and so convinced the young shortstop was a star in waiting he urged the Astros to make Jeter the No. 1 draftee in the nation. But the Astros had other ideas. They wanted someone closer to reaching the majors so they rejected Jeter, the high school kid, and opted for a college man, Phil Nevin.

The decision outraged Newhouser, who felt he was being slighted, his opinion disregarded and discounted. Being the honorable, regal, principled man of integrity that he was (they didn't call him "Prince Hal" for nothing), Newhouser resigned from the Astros and never worked in baseball again. Meanwhile, Jeter began the odyssey that would likely lead to the Hall of Fame, as the scout who recommended him to the Yankees had predicted.

Two years before, the Yankees had selected in the draft a slightly overweight eighteen-year-old left-handed pitcher of little renown from a junior college in the twenty-second round (Andy Pettitte) as well as a heavy-legged switch-hitting Puerto Rican second baseman from a little known community college in the twenty-fourth round (Jorge Posada). They had also signed a non-drafted free agent pitcher from the tiny fishing village of Puerto Caimito, Panama (Mariano Rivera).

As always, the Yankees entered the 1990 draft with left-handed pitchers as their highest priority. Toward that end they selected Kirt Ojala of the University of Michigan in the fourth round, Tim Rumer of Duke University in the eighth round, and Keith Seiler of the University of Virginia in the twenty-first round. In the twenty-second round, the Yankees opted for Andrew Eugene Pettitte from San Jacinto Junior College. All were left-handers.

Ojala, Rumer, and Seiler would combine to win three major league games (all by Ojala with the Florida Marlins). Pettitte would pitch in the major leagues for 18 seasons and win 219 games.

Two rounds after taking Pettitte, the Yankees selected Jorge Posada, a switch-hitting second baseman from Calhoun Community College whose uncle, Leo, was an outfielder for the Kansas City Athletics in the 1960s.

The number of prominent major leaguers from Panama can be counted on the fingers of one hand, so there wasn't much anticipation for Herb Raybourn, Director of Latin American Operations for the Yankees in 1990, when he got a tip about a young shortstop named Mariano Rivera in Puerto Caimito, Panama. Raybourn did his due diligence. He journeyed to the tiny fishing village, eyeballed the young shortstop, and submitted a report to the Yankees that would seem to condemn the youngster to the life of a fisherman—"He had good hands, but I didn't think he could be a major league shortstop, so I passed on him," Raybourn reported.

A year later, Raybourn got another tip. There was a kid pitcher in Puerto Caimito he was told he should see. The kid's name was Mariano Rivera. The name rang a bell.

"I know that name," Raybourn thought, "but he's a shortstop not a pitcher."

Nevertheless, Raybourn went back to Puerto Caimito to check out the young pitcher. Sure enough it was the same Mariano Rivera he had seen as a shortstop the previous year. What he saw this time was a skinny pitcher whose fastball registered a mere 84 miles an hour on the radar gun. But he also saw a kid who had a joy for the game, a strong desire to excel, a rare athleticism, and an easy, fluid pitching motion that caused the baseball to jump out of his hand and enable him to get good movement on his pitches.

It was enough for Raybourn to recommend to the Yankees that they sign the young pitcher, but he cautioned them not to spend too much to do so. The Yankees offered a modest signing bonus of $3,500. To a kid from Panama, faced with spending his life as a fisherman, it was a king's ransom.

Rivera was the first of the group to launch his professional career, starting in 1990 in the Gulf Coast rookie league. Pettitte and Posada began their careers the following year and Jeter the year after that, but it took him some time to catch up with the others. The four would not get together until the latter part of the 1994 season when they reached Columbus, the Yankees' top minor league affiliate in the AAA International League.

A year later they each made their major league debut, first Pettitte on April 29, Rivera twenty-five days later, Jeter six days after that, and Posada on September 4.

What are the chances that these four recruits would still be together as teammates more than two decades later, that they would share the success of seven American League pennants and five World Series, and that two of the four would be slam dunk first ballot Hall of Famers and that the other two would be on the fence but certainly in the Hall of Fame discussion?

They are an amorphous group, four men with little in common, four men from different parts of the world—Rivera from Panama; Posada, born in Puerto Rico; Pettitte, born in Louisiana and raised in Texas; and Jeter, born in New Jersey and raised in Michigan—of different ethnic backgrounds and different religions.

At some point they would be glorified as the "Core Four," but really they should be the Core Three—Rivera, Posada, and Jeter—who surpassed the record of Yount, Molitor, and Gantner and played together as teammates for seventeen consecutive seasons. (After the 2003 season Pettitte, a free agent, felt he needed to be home and spend more time with his young family. He could have retired, but instead he accepted a three-year $31.5 million offer from the Houston Astros and rationalized that at least he would be home half the time during the baseball season. After three years, Pettitte, apparently confident he had fulfilled his parental duty, returned to his adopted home and signed with the Yankees, where he remained through 2010.) Alternatively, they could have been the Core Five. (Bernie Williams was there when Rivera, Pettitte, and Posada arrived in 1995, comfortably ensconced for five years as the Yankees center fielder. He would retire following the 2006 season and pursue his avocation as a classical and jazz guitarist, but he was every bit as vital to the Yankees' success as Rivera, Jeter, Pettitte, and Posada.)

However, Core Three and Core Five doesn't have the pizzazz, the rhyme, or the ring to it, and so Core Four caught on and Core Four it remained until Posada retired after the 2011 season.

The breakup would be complete three years later with the retirement of Mariano Rivera in 2013 and Derek Jeter in 2014, each with a media extravaganza magical mystery farewell tour and culminated in an All-Star game pageantry.

Chosen to appear in his thirteenth All-Star game played in New York's Citi Field, Rivera, in recognition of his senior citizen status and his brilliant career, was asked to address the American League squad before the game.

"His speech was just about appreciation, how being a part of this game has meant so much to him," said Texas Rangers closer Joe Nathan. "It was very respectful, very classy. He could have talked about peanut butter and jelly and we all would have been like, 'Yeah, that's pretty cool.'"

The expectation, and the hope, was that the American League would have a lead in the ninth inning and would turn it over to "Mo" to do what he does better than anyone had ever done it. However, the AL manager Jim Leyland of the Detroit Tigers, a baseball purist and a thinking man, had given the various scenarios a lot of thought and was determined to make it a special moment. He was not going to take any chances. In addition to winning the game, Leyland's top priority was to make certain Rivera got in the game so that he could receive an appropriate farewell that befitted his stature and his singular career accomplishments. The American League scored a run in the top of the eighth to take a 3–0 lead, but Leyland feared that if the National

League scored 4 runs in the bottom of the eighth, there would be no save situation and, therefore, no Mo.

As the National League came to bat in the bottom of the eighth, the huge crowd was stunned to hear the strains of "Enter Sandman," Rivera's entrance song, and to see the bullpen door swing open and the familiar figure of Mariano Rivera jogging to the mound.

The crowd was on its feet greeting Rivera with a thunderous ovation. Rivera tipped his cap and then realized that there were no American League teammates manning their positions behind him and no National League batter getting ready to step up to the plate; the scene that had been carefully orchestrated by Leyland.

Players from both squads were on their feet in front of their respective dugouts, applauding along with the fans, and both bullpens had emptied and pitchers joined in the applause from the warning track.

When the cheers and tears had subsided, Rivera went about his business and retired the National League in order. There still was the ninth inning to be played and Nathan had the assignment. He held the NL scoreless and protected the victory for the save. At the time he had 341 regular season major league saves and he had saved the final ball from each of them, but he had never had a save in the All-Star game.

"I wanted it [the final ball]," Nathan said, but I wanted to give it to him [Rivera] more. It was a no-brainer. To be able to hand the ball over to him was pretty cool. It's no secret how much I look up to him and to be able to do that for him was awesome."

The accolades and the gifts continued to pour in on the Mariano Rivera Farewell Tour that would reach its crescendo on September 22, 2013, "Mariano Rivera Day" at Yankee Stadium.

The widow and daughter of Jackie Robinson were there to watch Rivera's No. 42 (Robinson's number) be permanently retired. Some years before Major League Baseball had decreed that the No. 42 would never be issued to another player, however all those already wearing the number would be grandfathered in and allowed to continue wearing it. Rivera was the last to do so.

Four days later the Yankees played their final game of the season—and the final game of Rivera's career—in Yankee Stadium against Tampa Bay. With the Rays leading 4–0 in the eighth inning, manager Joe Girardi called in Rivera to pitch. He got out of the inning and went out for the ninth. He retired the first two batters in the ninth and was preparing to face the third batter when he was startled to see Derek Jeter and Andy Pettitte headed his way.

It was the brain child of Girardi to have two of Mariano's Core Four compatriots go to the mound and remove Rivera from his final game in Yankee Stadium in order to give Mo one final raucous ovation from a grateful and adoring stadium crowd.

With three games remaining on the Yankees' schedule, all in Houston, Girardi gave Rivera the option of making the trip or not. Rivera slept on his decision and opted not to go to Houston in order to let his final game in Yankee Stadium be his adieu.

"I've had enough," he said.

Enough?

In his final season, at age forty-three, he had a record of 6–2, 44 saves in 50 save opportunities, an earned run average of 2.11, 54 strikeouts, and 17 walks in 64 innings.

Enough?

He left the game with 82 wins, a record 652 saves (not counting a 2–0 record and 18 saves in sixteen American League Division Series, a 4–0 record and 13 saves in thirteen American League Championship Series, and a 3–1 record and 11 saves in seven World Series), a 2.21 earned run average, 1,173 strikeouts, and 286 walks in 1,283⅔ innings.

While Rivera was going through a much-publicized farewell tour, meeting with team employees, stadium workers, and just fans in each city he visited, Pettitte was dealing with a dilemma. He had decided during spring training that 2013 would be his last season. His plan was to wait until all the hoopla attended to Rivera had died down and announce his retirement in the off-season so as not to rain on Mo's parade or make it appear he was hitching his wagon to a star.

It was Rivera who convinced Pettitte over lunch in Toronto to announce his retirement rather than wait until the offseason.

"You've got to announce it," Rivera admonished his friend. "You need to say something."

"He was so supportive," Pettitte said. "He said he thought it would make [Mariano Rivera Day] even better. "

And so it came to pass that September 22, 2013, turned into a dual celebration and Pettitte's inclusion in the festivities in no way intruded on the praises and accolades heaped upon Rivera.

As luck, and the schedule maker, would have it, the final three games of the Yankees season would be played in Houston on a Friday, Saturday, and Sunday in a ballpark twenty miles from Petitte's home in Deer Park, and Pettitte's final turn to pitch would come up on Saturday night.

With his mother, father, wife, four children, and more than fifty friends and neighbors in attendance, Pettitte pitched his heart out against the Astros, taking a 2–1 lead into the ninth inning. He had not pitched a complete game in seven years. He had not pitched one for the Yankees in ten years. But he retired the first two Astros in the ninth, gave up a single, and got the final out to finish the season with a record of 11–11 (in 18 major league seasons he never had a losing record). He would retire with 256 victories (at the time 42nd on the all-time list), and 2,448 strikeouts (36th on the all-time list at the time). As a Yankee he won 219 games, third behind Hall of Famers Whitey Ford and Red Ruffing, and he struck out 2,020 batters, No. 1 on the team's all-time list.

The tumult and shouting of the retirement pageantry of two members of the Yankees Core Four had hardly died down when the final member, Derek Jeter, announced that 2014 would be his final season. Thus began a year-round merry-go-round of tributes to arguably the greatest shortstop in baseball history. The whirlwind culminated in the All-Star Game in Minnesota. No doubt moved by sentiment and nostalgia, fans voted Jeter the American League's starting shortstop and the AL manager, John Farrell of the Yankees' archrival, the Boston Red Sox, penciled Jeter's name in the leadoff spot in his lineup.

But Jeter wasn't taking it all as ceremonial. His career had been based mostly on participating, performing, and winning. He hated taking a day off almost as much as he hated losing. As if to quiet the skeptics, he led off the bottom of the first with a double down the right field line and scored on a triple by Mike Trout, who has been ordained Jeter's successor as the face of baseball.

Jeter singled in the third, and when he went to his position in the top of the fourth he saw the White Sox's Alexei Ramirez headed his way. Jeter's all-star game career was over. He trotted into the American League dugout to a sustained standing ovation from the capacity crowd at Target Field. Once in the dugout, he went down the line and embraced everyone there.

The end would come for Derek Jeter some ten weeks later. He slipped into retirement as the only Yankee in their glorious history to record more than 3,000 hits, finishing with a total of

3,465 hits, sixth on baseball's revered all-time list. The five names ahead of him on that list will tell you all you need to know about Derek Jeter. Those names are Pete Rose (4,256); Ty Cobb (4,189); Henry Aaron (3,771); Stan Musial (3,630); and Tris Speaker (3,514).

Into their retirement, and beyond, Yankees fans debated Mariano Rivera and Derek Jeter's place in Yankees history. For years the so-called "Mount Rushmore" of Yankees consisted of Babe Ruth, Lou Gehrig, Joe DiMaggio, and Mickey Mantle. Now there was growing sentiment to include Rivera and Jeter in that quartet, but in whose place?

The debate figures to be ongoing for years, decades, maybe longer. But one thing seems certain: baseball never again will see the like of the Yankees' Core Four.

# TWENTY

# MY FRIEND THURMAN

I almost didn't get to know Thurman Munson—I mean the *real* Thurman Munson. I'm grateful I finally did.

I began my second tour as Yankees beat writer in 1971, the year after Munson was voted American League Rookie of the Year. In the five previous seasons, the Yankees had finished fifth, fifth, ninth, tenth, and sixth. Even though he was only twenty-three years old and a rookie, Thurman Munson was not going to stand for that. He batted .302 with 6 home runs and 53 runs batted in and displayed leadership that was well beyond his years. The Yankees won 93 games in Munson's rookie year and finished a distant second to the powerhouse Baltimore Orioles. It was improvement, and many saw it as the start of something good, but to Munson it was still second place, and that rendered his Rookie of the Year trophy as little consolation.

I soon discovered that along with being a fierce competitor Munson was a young curmudgeon, gruff, surly, ornery, and lacking a sense of humor, characteristics he came by naturally.

He was mostly uncooperative with the press, and even when he did make himself available, he seemed to answer questions with a chip on his shoulder. Nevertheless I found myself drawn to him, I believe, because of his vast knowledge of and his no-nonsense approach to the game. In short, he was a winner.

By 1974, the Yankees had become a legitimate contender. They finished in second place, two games behind Baltimore, and went into the 1975 season expected to make a run at a division title. But they reached the All-Star break in third place with a disappointing record of 45–41, 4½ games behind the Boston Red Sox.

To open the second half, the Yankees had a two-game series against the Texas Rangers in Arlington. They lost the first game, 7–2. Something had to be done. As the nominal leader of the team, Thurman Munson was the one to do it. (It would be a year later that he was formally named team captain by owner George Steinbrenner, and when someone reminded Steinbrenner that the Yankees hadn't had a captain since Lou Gehrig and that they had not only permanently retired the ill-fated Gehrig's No. 4, but they also announced there would never be another Yankees captain, the Boss replied, "I'm sure that if Lou Gehrig knew Thurman Munson he would approve of this decision.") The following afternoon he called a players-only meeting in which anyone could air his gripe outside the presence of the manager Bill Virdon and his coaches, the idea being to get some things off their chest in order to get the ship turned in the right direction.

As so often happens in such cases, there was a leak from a player (not Munson) who told me about the meeting, so I wrote about it for the *Daily News*, emphasizing that the meeting was all Munson's idea and he did most of the talking. Back in New York a friend of Munson's read the story and called Thurman to tell him what was in the paper. Munson went ballistic on me. How dare I violate his confidence and write such a thing?

I argued that not only was I just doing my job (that old standby), but that the story didn't present him in a negative light. On the contrary, it showed leadership; it showed that he cared and that he had the courage to put it all on the line to help turn things around. My argument was in vain. I found out first-hand then and there that there was no arguing with Thurman Munson. What's more, he made it clear that he was cutting me off. He vowed never to talk to me again. Never, I fretted, is a long time.

I rationalized that there still were twenty-four other players who were talking to me, or so I believed.

For the rest of the '75 season and most of '76 Munson ignored me while the Yankees were steamrolling the American League on their way to their first American League pennant in a dozen years. Meanwhile I found I had enough sources so I wasn't deprived by being cold-shouldered by the player his teammates called "Squatty Body."

Munson was having a sensational season, sporting a batting average that hovered around .300, double figures in home runs, and close to 100 RBI with a small portion left in the season. More than that, he had taken charge as the team leader. His defense was superb. Behind the plate he had catlike reflexes and although his arm was just average, he had a lightning-quick release that gunned down potential base stealers or picked unsuspecting runners off base. In addition he was a brilliant signal caller with a seemingly photographic memory that cat-alogued opponents' batting strengths and weaknesses, and he excelled in coaxing, cajoling, and badgering pitchers (most of them older and more experienced than he) into raising their performance and competitiveness.

By midseason Munson was being touted as the likely American League Most Valuable Player. But there were other worthy candidates—George Brett and Hal McRae of the Kansas City Royals; Rod Carew of the Minnesota Twins, the perennial American League batting champion; and Munson's own teammates Chris Chambliss and Mickey Rivers—and the debate about which was the most worthy raged on through the summer.

At some point my sports editor asked me if I had an opinion on who should be the AL Most Valuable Player. I said I did, and he suggested I write a column stating who my choice was and why. Since I was not selected that year to serve on the committee voting for the American League MVP, I figured there was no conflict of interest in writing that column.

My choice for Most Valuable Player, I wrote, was Mickey Rivers. I have always maintained that the Most Valuable Player is not necessarily the season's best player. The name of the award tells us that. The award is Most Valuable Player, not Player of the Year, which to me means that the award is earmarked for that player without whom his team would not be as successful. My interpretation is that it pretty much means the Most Valuable Player should come from a winning team, preferably a championship team (although votes are to be submitted prior to the start of the postseason).

Rivers had come to the Yankees in a trade with the California Angels that winter, and his impact on the team was immediate and obvious. He provided an element the Yankees had rarely possessed, speed. It enabled Rivers to cover the vast expanse of center field, to represent a base-stealing threat, and to force the defense to guard against a bunt, thereby giving Rivers the opportunity to slap hits past infielders, a skill he perfected and at which he was most proficient .

Rivers proved to be an excellent clutch hitter and one gifted with surprising power for someone his size (five feet, ten inches, 165 pounds). As a leadoff batter and with his speed, he was the catalyst that ignited the Yankees and sparked them to 97 wins, a bump of 14 over the previous year.

It was this combination of factors that motivated me to write that I believed the Yankees 1976 Most Valuable Player, indeed the American League's Most Valuable Player, was Mickey Rivers.

The day the column ran, I reported to Yankee Stadium as usual and was roaming around the clubhouse, chitchatting with players (with one exception) when the exception, who hadn't spoken to me in almost a year, accosted me, a circumstance I had been anticipating.

"I just want to ask you one question," Munson said. "Did you write that column because I'm not talking to you, or do you really believe it?"

"Thurman," I said, "I may not always succeed, but I try not to let my personal feelings or relationships enter into my opinion. No, I wrote it because I think Rivers has been the major difference between this year's team and last year's."

"That's all I wanted to know," Munson said, and he walked away, apparently satisfied with my reply.

I thought that would be the end of it, but it wasn't. Miraculously, there suddenly was a change in Munson's attitude toward me. From that day forward, he began talking to me and acting as if nothing negative had ever happened between us.

Munson wound up winning the 1976 American League Most Valuable Player award in a landslide over George Brett. Munson received eighteen first-place votes of the twenty-four votes cast and a total of 304 points (voters picked ten players in order of preference, and points were awarded on a descending basis from one to ten). Brett received two first-place votes and 217 points. My guy, Mickey Rivers, got one first-place vote and 179 points.

The next time I saw Munson, I congratulated him on winning the award and made some snide comment about eighteen voters not knowing what they were doing.

As time went on our relationship grew and strengthened to the point where I could get away with sarcastic comments to the king of sarcasm, because I certainly had to endure more than my share of sarcasm from him.

I even took the liberty of taking little digs at Thurman in print. When the Yankees brought catcher Brad Gulden up from the minor leagues, I wrote, "The Yankees had the hot dog (Reggie Jackson) and the sour kraut (Thurman Munson) and now they have the mustard (Brad Gulden)."

Not only did Thurman not take offense at the remark, but rather he said he liked it.

The first hint I had that our relationship had changed for the better was that Thurman would give me little bits of information that helped me in my work. As an example, we were chatting one day and he said, "Have you ever noticed that with their first pitch of the game Figgy [Ed Figueroa] and TJ [Tommy John] always throw a curve ball?"

It was a harmless tidbit that I made certain to follow whenever Figuroa or John pitched, but I interpreted it as a sign of his growing trust in me.

And he advised me when I went to him to recommend the proper beginner's catcher's mitt I should buy for Jim, my No. 2

son (that's his chronological place, not a rating), who decided to go out for his high school baseball team as a catcher.

Munson reached into his locker, where there were about a half dozen catcher's mitts piled up, took one down, and handed it to me.

I pulled out my notebook and began writing down numbers.

"What are you doing?" Munson asked.

"I'm writing the serial number so I can buy the right mitt," I explained.

"You're not buying any mitt," Munson said, gruffly. "Take it. It's yours."

"Well, at least let me pay you for it."

"The company sends them to me because I use their gloves. I get as many as I want. I don't pay for them and neither do you."

At the end of one season I asked Munson for his home telephone so that I could reach him in the offseason if I needed him.

"I don't give out my home phone number," he said. "Especially to sportswriters!"

"You're the captain of this team," I argued, effectively, I thought. "That means you speak for the players. Something may come up that you're going to want to comment on and nobody will be able to reach you."

My arguments seemed to register with Mr. Personality, because he reneged. He asked for my notebook and pen and wrote down a series of numbers.

"This is my father-in-law's phone number," he said. "His name is Tony. You call him and tell him you want to talk to me and why and leave your number and he will call me and tell me you called and then if I want to call you back I will. If I don't want to call you back I won't."

A few weeks passed and something came up, I can't remember what, but it required a comment from Mr. Charm. So I followed his instructions and called Tony, a cordial man, and explained that I needed to talk with Thurman. I asked him to have Munson call me in my office and gave him the number.

"Tell him to call collect," I said magnanimously.

About an hour later, the phone rang. I picked it up and the voice practically shouted into my ear, "WHAT THE (BLEEP) DO YOU WANT?"

"I told Tony that you should call me collect," I admonished.

"Look, stupid," he said endearingly. "If I called you collect, I'd have to talk to the operator and she's going to ask for my name and then it might get out and people will know that I called a sportswriter and there goes my reputation."

Early one spring morning in 1979 I was on duty covering the Yankees spring training in Fort Lauderdale. I walked into the clubhouse and Munson caught my eye and signaled for me to go to his locker. I figured he had some piece of news he wanted to pass along. Instead I was floored when he said, "I heard your marriage broke up, and I want to know how you're getting along."

"I appreciate you asking, Thurman. I'm doing all right. My three older kids are teenagers in high school so they have their own activities to keep them busy. And they're accustomed to me being away from home this time of year. It's my little guy I'm concerned about. He's only four years old so he doesn't know what's going on, but he misses his daddy and I miss him."

"Why don't you bring him down here?"

"It would be tough having him here and doing my job, which sometimes keeps me occupied at all hours."

"You can hire someone to look after him when you're working."

"You don't get it, Thurman," I said. "I'm a sportswriter. Not a ballplayer. We don't make enough money to afford something like that."

"Listen," he said, looking me straight in the eye, his voice dropping into a lower register, his words emphatic, even insistent. "If you need money to bring your son down here, you have it. All you have to do is ask."

I was blown away by such generosity and more important by such compassion from a man I had always thought either lacked feelings or the courage to reveal his feelings.

Coincidentally, at the time, like my youngest child, John, Thurman's youngest of three children and his only boy Michael was four years old. Munson had chosen not to disrupt his children's schooling by moving them to New Jersey during the baseball season, so he took up flying. He purchased a Cessna Citation with the objective that he would use it to fly home at every opportunity.

He often talked about how he found peace flying solo, and he boasted how he was able to sneak home during the season to be with his family. If the Yankees had a day off at home, Thurman would leave Yankee Stadium after the last out, drive to Teterboro Airport, get in his private plane, and fly to his home in Ohio. He bragged that he would be home in Canton not much later than he would get home to New Jersey after a game.

At home he could spend the off day with his kids or conduct business, and the following day he would fly back to Teterboro and make it to Yankee Stadium in time for pregame practice.

In a television interview with the former Yankees shortstop Tony Kubek, Munson rhapsodized about his love of flying.

"I think it's great, the feeling of being alone for an hour or two by yourself. You're up there and nobody asks any questions.

You don't have to put on any kind of an act. You just go up there and enjoy yourself. You have to be on your toes, but it's just a kind of relaxation when you spend a lot of time by yourself, and I need that. I also need to get home a lot, so I love to fly."

In his eleventh major league season, Munson was beginning to sense the mortality of his professional life. There were run-ins with the Yankees owner George Steinbrenner that caused Munson to talk about asking to be traded to the Cleveland Indians so that he could be closer to his home.

At the same time there was concern about Munson's physical condition and fears that his days as a catcher were coming to an end. The years of squatting behind the plate had taken their toll on the cantankerous catcher. Munson began shagging fly balls in right field in compliance with the plan that Thurman would slip into the role of part-time catcher and turn most of the catching responsibilities to a consortium of the veteran Cliff Johnson and youngsters Jerry Narron and Brad Gulden. In order to keep his bat in the lineup, Munson would play most of the time in right field replacing Reggie Jackson, who would become the Yankees' full-time designated hitter. Munson's teammates viewed these changes as weakening the Yankees both offensively and defensively.

The severity of Munson's condition had not yet surfaced as the 1979 season reached the halfway mark and the Yankees embarked on an exhausting ten-day West Coast trip that would take them to Oakland, Seattle, and Anaheim just before the All-Star game. Munson would catch eight of the ten games, including both games of a doubleheader in Oakland.

On Saturday, July 14, the day before the final game of the trip, the Yankees played a night game against the Angels in Anaheim. In the sixth inning, the irascible Munson surfaced. He was called out on strikes by plate umpire Fred Spenn, and he let the arbiter know, in no uncertain terms, what he thought of Spenn's eyesight, his umpiring ability, his ancestry, and his pet dog. Munson was retired for the night, but he left with the Yankees in good hands, leading by the score of 6–0.

With Munson out, the Angels rallied, tied the score, and beat the Yankees, 8–7 in twelve innings.

After the game, I wrote my story, filed it, and joined a couple of my colleagues for a quick snack. It was about 11 p.m. when I returned to the hotel and went to the hotel's convenience store to pick up a newspaper, and who should I see there but my favorite curmudgeon. I watched as he grabbed a bag of potato chips, a bag of pretzels, a bag of Fritos, and a few other packages of nutrition.

"What are you doing?" I asked.

"I missed dinner," he said. "I'm hungry."

"Don't eat that stuff," I chastised. "There's a hamburger joint right up the street. Why don't you go there?"

"I hate eating alone," he said.

"I'll come and sit with you. I'm not ready for sleep yet anyway."

"You will?" he said, surprised.

"Yeah! I think I can stand being with you for a few minutes."

We talked for hours, about family, things apart from baseball. Eventually, the subject of his flying came up and he spoke animatedly of the love of his new hobby. He even offered to take me for a ride as his passenger.

"No way," I said. "I'm not going flying with you. I'll stick to flying with the experts and professionals."

"You don't have to worry. It's perfectly safe. Look, I don't care if you live or die, but I certainly care if I live or die."

Nineteen days later Thurman Munson was killed when his Cessna Citation crashed as he was practicing takeoffs and landings at Canton-Akron Airport.

Naturally, I was shocked and devastated on the one hand. On the other, I was a professional journalist and I had a job to do, so I immersed myself in that job, telephoning his teammates for their reaction and then sitting down to write my story. At that point, there seemed to be no time for mourning.

# TWENTY-ONE

# OFF MY CHEST

I have a bee in my bonnet, a fly in my ointment, a bat in my belfry. Having followed or reported on baseball for seven decades I have seen it all (almost) and I have reached the age where I can vent my spleen and rail at my pet peeves with impunity. Age really does bring privilege.

I will now unburden myself of the bee, the fly, and the bat and do so at the risk of flying in the face of conventional baseball wisdom and of being scorned, shunned, and possibly drummed out of the Baseball Writers Association of America as a heretic and a curmudgeon who has taken leave of his senses.

It's time to come out of the closet and own up to the fact that I do not follow lamblike the pronouncements of the so-called baseball cognoscenti that maintain pitching wins championships. I cannot in good faith nod my head at such pronouncements or worship at the shrine of those that make them.

When I hear those self-proclaimed baseball Einsteins pontificate that "Good pitching will stop good hitting"—a canard born out of the dead ball era, which is just that, dead—am I sup-posed to nod in agreement when what I am really thinking is "and vice versa?"

When I hear one of those geniuses say, "If your pitcher throws a shutout, you can't lose," do I submit in supplication when what I am really tempted to respond is "and if your offense does not score a run, you can't *win.*"

So at the risk of being forced to broadcast my ignorance by wearing a scarlet letter (I suppose that letter is an "E" for error) I will press on in an attempt to fight the good fight.

I'm not fool enough to think you can win championships without pitching and defense, especially in this day of multi-tiered playoffs (the shorter the series, the more important the pitching). But why are *they* fool enough to think you can get to the playoffs without hitting?

Let's examine some of baseball's great dynasties—the '27 Yankees; the '39 Yankees; the '61 Yankees; Cincinnati's Big Red Machine; the Cardinals' Gas House Gang; the Oakland Athletics of 1972–73–74, and their younger brothers of 1988–89–90; the Pittsburgh Pirates of the early 1970s; the Philadelphia Athletics from 1910 to 1915; and the Detroit Tigers of 1907–08–09.

I know all those teams had excellent pitching, some even including Hall of Famers. But what is the common denominator that binds them? What is the attribute that defines them? I submit it's their ability to bludgeon the opposition into submission.

Why are the '27 Yankees of Ruth, Gehrig, Lazzeri, and Meusel known as Murderers' Row and not Pitchers' Parade? (I challenge you to name three hurlers from that team.)

Why, when we think about the '39 Yankees, is it the name Joe DiMaggio that we reference?

Why do we associate the 1961 Yankees with M&M (Mantle and Maris) and not F&A (Ford and Arroyo)?

Why are they the Bronx Bombers and not the Bronx Bowlers?

Cincinnati's Big Red Machine refers to a star-studded everyday lineup of Johnny Bench, Pete Rose, Joe Morgan, et al., not to a well-oiled pitching staff. In his nine-year run as manager of the Machine, Sparky Anderson had only *one* 20-game winner, but he had three Hall of Famers and one guy named Pete who should be in the Hall of Fame.

The St. Louis Cardinals of the 1930s were defined not by the pitching of the Dean Brothers (Dizzy and Daffy), but by the hell-for-leather, flying spikes, and clenched fist style of play of "the Wild Horse of the Osage," Pepper Martin; the "Fordham Flash" Frankie Frisch; Ripper Collins; Leo (the Lip) Durocher; and Joe Medwick, all members in good standing of the "Gashouse Gang."

The Oakland Athletics of 1972–74 had Reggie Jackson, Joe Rudi, and Sal Bando; the A's of 1988–90 had the Bash Brothers—Jose Canseco and Mark McGwire.

The Pittsburgh Pirates, which won six division titles and two World Series in the decade of the 1970s, were known as "the Lumber Company," led by "Pops," Willie Stargell.

In their early days in Philadelphia, the Athletics of Connie Mack dominated the American League, winning four pennants and three World Series in a five-year stretch from 1910–14. Those Athletics were powered by the so-called "$100,000 infield" that included third baseman Frank "Home Run" Baker, who earned his nickname by leading the league in home runs for four straight years with 11, 10, 12, and 9.

Prior to the Athletics' dominance, the Detroit Tigers won three consecutive American League pennants led by a young center fielder named Tyrus Raymond (Ty) Cobb, who would win twelve American League batting championships and finish with a lifetime average of .366, the highest in baseball history.

The strongest argument for the hitter vs. pitcher debate, however, comes from a young man with the Boston Red Sox who had a three-year stretch in which he won 65 games and lost only 33, a winning percentage of .663, had pitched 106 complete games and 16 shutouts by the age of twenty-three, and was regarded as the finest left-handed pitcher in the league. Nevertheless, the Red Sox thought so much of his thunderous bat that they were willing to sacrifice a potential Hall of Fame career as a pitcher in order to capitalize on the young man's awesome power.

That young man's name was George Herman Ruth, "the Babe."

## WHATEVER BECAME OF THE FIRST BALL CEREMONY?

When I was a boy, and until about a couple of decades or so ago, usually on opening day but also on special occasions, baseball had a wonderful popular tradition called the "first ball ceremony." The idea was to have a dignitary—hopefully the president of the United States; or at least a popular celebrity from show business, television, or the movies; a former player; or even a carefully selected fan—toss a baseball to a player from the home team prior to the start of the game, thereby symbolizing that the teams now had a baseball and could begin play: no ball, no game! As in, "If you don't let me play, I'm going to take my ball and go home."

The first ball ceremony, like pitchers going nine innings and hitters remaining in the batters' box after each pitch, is a thing of a past. It has gone the way of ticker tape, telephone booths, and phonograph records, replaced by a stranger known as the "first pitch" ceremony.

I don't know for certain when this change took place. I suspect it was on or about Opening Day in 1993 when President Bill Clinton decided that rather than throw the ball from a box seat near the home team dugout (as every first-ball-throwing president since William Taft had done), he was going to make his delivery from above or just in front of the pitcher's mound in order to gain maximum exposure and at the same time display his virility and baseball talent. So it's likely that from that day on, it became the "first pitch ceremony," the rationale being that because it was made from the pitcher's mound it was a "pitch," which it was not.

The dictionary defines a pitch as the act of throwing a baseball toward a batter at home plate to start a play. But there is no batter when a president or a celebrity or any other dignitary throws out the "first ball." So how can that be a pitch?

Therefore I will continue to swim against the tide and maintain it's a "first ball ceremony."

## KEEPING SCORE

I have been an official scorer, and as such I have gained enormous respect for those who do this job on Major League Baseball's behalf. For the most part I have found these persons to be dedicated, conscientious, fair-minded, honest, trustworthy, and impartial. So it is not the scorers that I criticize here but rather the rules under which they are forced to operate and which they don't control.

I have long been a proponent of the "team error" and remain mystified why such a concept continues to be excluded from the scoring rules. To wit:

A batter hits a high, lazy pop fly to "no man's land," the Bermuda Triangle of baseball, too shallow for the right fielder (or center fielder), too deep for the second baseman (or first baseman or shortstop), and the ball falls to the ground untouched. Invariably, because he is unable to assign culpability to any fielder for failing to catch an easy pop fly, the official scorer "credits" the batter with a hit, which the batter has not earned. Common sense cries out for the injustice of such a decision. Ask yourself these questions.

Did the batter, after hitting the pop fly, think he had a great at-bat and congratulate himself for beating the pitcher? Or did he mentally slam his bat down in disgust for failing to square up the pitch and hit a seed?

Is it fair that while the fielders and the hitter get off free, the only player being penalized is the one person who did his job, the pitcher?

The "team error" not only protects the pitcher, but also it refuses to reward the batter for hitting a lazy pop up and it does not force the official scorer to ascribe culpability to any specific fielder. It seems a basic long overdue solution to an injustice.

Here's another hypothetical situation that has irked me for years. It's the top of the ninth inning and the team at bat is trailing by 7 or 8 runs. They get a runner to third with less than two outs and the next batter hits a fly ball to the outfield. The runner from third scores, and the batter returns to his dugout and is greeted by the customary congratulatory fist bump—traditionally the acknowledgment of a successful time at-bat—as if he purposely tried to hit an outfield fly to bring home a run with his team down by seven or eight.

Worse, for his effort the batter is not only rewarded with a run batted in, but also he is not charged with an at-bat, thereby protecting his batting average.

Compare that with another situation. It's late in a game, say the seventh, eighth, or ninth inning. The team at bat is behind by one run. It gets a man to third with less than two outs. The team in the field chooses to play its infield back and the batter hits a groundball that scores the tying run.

Like the previous example, the batter is rewarded with a run batted in. However, unlike the previous example, despite giving himself up and knocking in the tying run, the batter *is* charged with a time at bat. Talk about an unjust rule!

And speaking of injustice, here's another example. It's the ninth inning and the team in the field is ahead by 4 or 5 runs. The team at bat gets a runner on first, but as has become the custom, the first baseman does not hold the runner on base. Consequently, the runner on first takes off for second and makes it safely without a throw. The ruling is no stolen base because of "defensive indifference."

Fair enough!

However, the runner on second eventually scores on a single. Clearly he would not have scored from first on the hit, yet the pitcher is penalized by being charged with an earned run when by the very definition of the term "defensive indifference," there never was any attempt to prevent the runner from going from first base to second.

## TO DH OR NOT TO DH

I am enough of a baseball traditionalist and a dinosaur to admit that I prefer the National League game to the American League game, but I also appreciate the designated hitter because it has allowed me to see the best of Edgar Martinez, one of the greatest right-handed hitters I ever watched; David Ortiz, the best clutch hitter of his time; the magical Paul Molitor; the Big Hurt Frank Thomas; the underappreciated Harold Baines; the thorough professionalism of Victor Martinez; and the graceful and dignified Andre Thornton.

## BROADCAST NEWS

I continue to be baffled by the language of baseball as employed by those practitioners of the art, the ones who broadcast the games. I sometimes find myself wondering what language they're speaking. Why doesn't Berlitz offer a course in the language of baseball? An epidemic of word pollution abounds on the airwaves, especially during baseball season. The pervading sentiment in the booth appears to be there's no reason to use three words to get your point across when thirty-three will do quite nicely.

I cringed at the words of the baseball broadcaster who said a certain team made "an inning-ending triple play," and the one who said, "The oldest man to pitch a no-hitter in the major leagues was Nolan Ryan, who was forty-four when he pitched his no-hitter against the Toronto Blue Jays. It was the last of his seven no-hitters."

Why do sportscasters say Smith "could care less" when what they really mean to say is Smith "couldn't care less," which means he cares as little as possible while "could care less" means he cares quite a bit?

And why do these same sportscasters say, "Let's see if the Bears can't score a run off Smith," when what they mean is "Let's see if the Bears *can* score a run off Smith." (We already have evidence that they can't score a run off Smith.)

Why do baseball broadcasters say, "Jones retired the first six batters he faced" when he could only retire the batters he *faced* not the ones he didn't face, and why do broadcasters say that same pitcher Jones has retired "the last six batters in a row" when if he retired the last six batters they had to be in a *row*, didn't they?

There seems to be an obsession among baseball broadcasters with the word "on." Consequently we learn that an infielder waits "on" a groundball and a batter waits "on" a pitch (a waiter or waitress in a restaurant waits "on" a customer, but people wait "for" a train, infielders wait "for" a grounder, and batters wait "for" a pitch); batters are said to swing "on" a pitch (one swings "on" a hammock or "on" a rope tied to a tree, but a batter swings "at" a pitch); we are told ad nauseam that Joe Blow has 14 home runs "on" the season, Jim Smith has 8 strikeouts "on" the game, and Tom Tough has 2,500 hits "on" his career when the truth is Joe Blow has 14 home runs "for" the season, Jim Smith has 8 strikeouts "in" the game, and Tom Tough has 2,500 hits "for" his career.

I suppose to explain the preponderance of the word one can only conclude that there are more "ons" in the broadcast booths of Major League Baseball.

I recently heard a sportscaster say, "Babe Ruth may be dead, but his legacy will live forever."

*May* be dead? Where has this guy been? Hasn't he heard? Babe Ruth died on August 16, 1948. It was in all the papers.

The sportscaster went on to say that Babe would probably hit 70 or 80 home runs today. I say nonsense. The Babe would probably hit about 25–30 home runs today.

"Only twenty-five to thirty?" you say.

That's right. After all, the Babe would be about 120 years old today.

We are being bombarded with a barrage of superfluity coming out of our television. Why, for instance, must we repeatedly hear "the Yankees are playing their *first ever* game in the new Yankee Stadium" as if including the word "ever" makes it more important, earlier, and more emphatic? If we were told simply that the Yankees are playing their first game in the new Yankee Stadium, would anyone listening not understand that the Yankees had never before played a game in the new Yankee Stadium?

Why must broadcasters say that John Brown's 46 home runs are second only to Bob White? If he's second to Bob White than the words "only to" are superfluous. Or "Jack Sprat is expected to return to the lineup as early as tomorrow." Isn't it enough to say "Jack Sprat is expected to return to the lineup tomorrow?" How does the phrase "as early as" change the meaning of the message?

I am also baffled by what is meant by broadcasters who say the throw to second base was "not nearly in time." What exactly does "not nearly in time" mean?

And when a pitcher gives up a couple of hits, or a walk and a hit, but strikes out three batters in the inning, why do announcers say the pitcher has "struck out the side?" No, he didn't. He struck out three batters, but the "side" also had a couple of hits or a walk and a hit.

I also take exception to the baseball broadcaster who tells us that a right-handed batter dropped a drag bunt. Just as only a boxer in a right-handed stance can throw a left hook and only a boxer in a left-handed stance can throw a right hook, *only* a left-handed hitter can execute a drag bunt, which occurs when the left-handed batter bunts a ball toward the right side as he leaves the batter's box (i.e., he drags the ball with him, and therefore it's a drag bunt). Conversely, a right-handed batter cannot drag a bunt with him as he heads to first base.

Finally, I wonder how we ever got baseball games started back in the day without the go-ahead provided by Totalers Tea, Aromatic Bread, various and sundry automobile companies, insurance providers, and fast food restaurants that graciously favor us with good weather, allow us to present the starting lineup, and give the home team pitcher permission to make the game's first pitch. What would we do without their munificent gifts? Would the games have to be canceled?

So in the interest of truth and giving the proper sponsors their due, I suggest that in the future some intrepid baseball broadcaster announced the following:

"Today's starting lineup is brought to you by Henry Chadwick.

The first pitch of today's game is sponsored by our good friend William Howard Taft.

The defensive alignment is brought to you by Gen. George C. Marshall.

And today's weather is brought to you by God."

## MANAGING TO WIN

Tony LaRussa, Joe Torre, and Bobby Cox won the staggering combined total of 7,558 major league games, 17 pennants, and eight World Series as a manager—Hall of Fame–worthy résumés. They got their due recently when they were enshrined in Cooperstown.

But what about the story behind the story?

While there is no evidence that Cox benefitted from players charged with or accused of using performance-enhancing drugs, the same cannot be said for LaRussa and Torre.

LaRussa's résumé was enhanced no small measure by the booming bats of Jose Canseco and Mark McGwire. Torre's record is marred because his success in part was built on the backs of Roger Clemens, Jason Giambi, Alex Rodriguez, Andy Pettitte, and Melky Cabrera.

The defense that the managers had no way of knowing what their players were doing and therefore they are not complicit in any wrongdoing does not wash. One of the reasons these men were so successful and reportedly made them Hall of Fame–caliber managers is that they controlled their clubhouse. So how can we truly believe they had no knowledge what was going on in their house?

The players mentioned above who reached Hall of Fame eligibility had their chances short-circuited, I'm proud to say, by the voters of the Baseball Writers Association of America. In their first year of eligibility Clemens received only 35.4 percent of the vote and McGwire 11.0 percent of the vote (75 percent is needed for election). Canseco received only six votes in his first year, 2006, and since he failed to get at least 5 percent of the vote, his name has been removed from the ballot. Clearly the writers turned thumbs down on those players they knew, or believed, cheated to achieve success.

The members of the BBWAA, incidentally, were not involved in the vote that confirmed the election of the three managers. Still, the question remains, if McGwire and Clemens have been snubbed by the BBWAA panel of Hall of Fame electors, should baseball have honored and ennobled the managers who may have enabled them?

Just asking!